HOME OFFICE RESEARCH STUDY NO. 107

G000037978

Domestic Violence: an overview of the literature

by Lorna J. F. Smith

A HOME OFFICE
RESEARCH AND PLANNING UNIT
REPORT

LONDON: HMSO

HOME OFFICE RESEARCH STUDIES

"Home Office Research Studies" comprise reports on research undertaken in the Home Office to assist in the exercise of its administrative functions, and for the information of the judicature, the services for which the Home Secretary has responsibility (direct or indirect) and the general public.

On the last pages of this report are listed titles already published in this series, in the preceding series Studies in the Causes of Delinquency and the Treatment of Offenders, and in the series of Research and Planning Unit Papers.

Her Majesty's Stationery Office

Standing order service

Placing a standing order with HMSO BOOKS enables a customer to receive other titles in this series automatically as published.

This saves time, trouble and expense of placing individual orders and avoids the problem of knowing when to do so.

For details please write to HMSO BOOKS (PC13A/1), Publications Centre, PO Box 276, London, SW8 5DT and quoting reference X25.08.07.

The standing order service also enables customers to receive automatically as published all material of their choice which additionally saves extensive catalogue research. The scope and selectivity of the service has been extended by new techniques, and there are more than 3,500 classifications to choose from. A special leaflet describing the service in detail may be obtained on request.

Foreword

Violent crime has always given rise to particular concern; that which occurs within the family setting is no less distressing than any other and has over the past two decades or so received increasing attention.

This report reviews the now extensive literature which exists on the topic of domestic violence. It presents evidence as to the extent and nature of the problem and discusses the explanations which have been advanced to account for its occurrence. Legal remedies and their application in practice are described, as are the responses of statutory and other agencies in dealing with domestic violence and how those responses are perceived by victims.

The research reviewed shows that there are no easy solutions to this multi-faceted problem. Nevertheless, the lessons that have been learned from existing studies and from the experience of other countries are fully discussed in the hope that this will not only make a contribution towards a better understanding of this type of crime, but also to any consideration of how it might be most effectively tackled.

MARY TUCK
Head of Research and Planning Unit
January 1989

Acknowledgements

I should like to express my thanks to my colleagues Peter Southgate and Roger Tarling for their unfailing support and encouragement.

LORNA J. F. SMITH

Contents

1 Problematic terminology

Domestic violence, family violence, domestic disputes, spouse abuse, wife abuse, woman abuse, battered wives, battered women... There is a plethora of terms which are used, sometimes almost interchangeably, to describe the same phenomenon. Often they serve to confuse rather than to clarify. In this report it is proposed to use the term 'domestic violence'[1] despite criticisms which have been made that it masks who is the victim and who the perpetrator (see, for example, Morris, 1987). In the last two decades, the research literature on domestic violence has grown considerably. Much of that literature stems from North America but there is an increasing number of studies from the United Kingdom. Interest in the subject has been shown by a variety of disciplines: psychology, sociology, law, medicine, social work and criminology. The problem is also now receiving considerable public attention as revealed, for example, by increasing press coverage. The lessons to be learned from research are, however, scattered through numerous textbooks and academic journals. This review was undertaken both to inform public debate and to provide a readily accessible source of information for further research by pulling together in one volume the diverse strands of various research endeavours and critically reviewing their results. The provision of such information also facilitates the scrutiny of existing policy and the planning of future directions. The retention of the term 'domestic violence' is partly, therefore, but only partly, a matter of convenience. In policy-making circles, 'domestic violence' is the term in common usage.

But retention of the term 'domestic violence' also helps to emphasise — in a way that the terms 'abuse' and 'disputes' do not — that what is being examined *is* violence, not arguments or minor altercations, but violence. Domestic violence, as will be shown, can be of a serious and prolonged nature, escalating in frequency and intensity over time. In the United States, for example, the 1986 Special Report of the Bureau of Justice Statistics estimated that half of the domestic 'simple assaults' actually involved bodily injury as serious as or more serious than ninety per cent of all rapes, robberies and aggravated assaults. The term 'domestic violence' is not used in this report in a pejorative way, to connote that it is somehow different from, less serious than, or less of a problem than other forms of violence. Rather, the retention of 'domestic' is deliberate to underline that we are talking about violence which occurs within the context of marriage or cohabitation — in a setting which Pahl (1985) — borrowing Lasch's (1977) oft quoted phrase —

[1] Other forms of intra-familial violence, for example, child abuse and abuse of elderly relatives are not included in this review which is concerned with the violence occurring between partners living as a couple, whether married or co-habiting.

1

describes as generally being perceived as "a safe haven in a heartless world". Wilson (1983) identifies the paradox: the place to which most people run "to get away from fear and violence" can be, for women, the context of "the most frightening violence of all". Domestic violence arguably *is* special, yet it is special not because somehow it does not matter so much but rather because it perhaps matters *more*.

It has been suggested that the terms "disputes" and "abuse" can underplay the violence involved and thus serve to mask or trivialise the problem. To talk of battered women or battered wives is at once both too wide and too narrow. The former, despite its popular use, could be criticised for its possible ambiguity — for failing to distinguish adequately that the violence occurs within the context of private relationships — whilst the latter might be taken to preclude relationships falling outside the marriage contract. Both preclude the possibility of men being victims: the term "domestic violence" does not. The retention of domestic violence, therefore, accepts that both women and men can be victims and perpetrators. Nevertheless, it has to be stressed at the outset that most studies show that it is, in the main, women who are the victims of violence, men who are the aggressors. Moreover, it is women who bear the brunt of serious injury (see, for example, Straus *et al*. 1980; Loving and Farmer, 1980; Dobash and Dobash, 1979). Pahl (1985) has pointed out that it is significant that the term "battered wives" is used rather than "violent husbands". It shifts attention away from the instigators of the violence and onto its victims, thus encouraging a search for solutions among the victims themselves rather than among their attackers. Although this emphasis may aid short-term solutions, she argues that any long-term solution will have to address the problem more accurately described as "violent husbands". Again, the term "domestic violence" embraces this concept.

2 Historical perspectives

Domestic violence is by no means a new phenomenon though its development as a recognised social problem has a very uneven history (see, for example, Pleck, 1987). Freeman (1980) thinks that its recognition as such tends to coincide with periods in which an active "feminist movement has flourished or at least been sufficiently vocal to bring it to public attention". Nor has its study received systematic attention in the academic world (Couch, 1983), including criminology where it has often been characterised as a problem of victims rather than examined in, for example, explorations of crime causation (Morash, 1986).

Martin (1978) described the historical roots of wife beating as ancient and deep, going back to the first monogamous pairing relationships which, she contended, brought about the subjugation of one sex by another. This subjugation of women to their husbands was sanctioned by the church and wives counselled that increased devotion and submissiveness were the means of avoiding "disciplinary" chastisement. One of the earliest reported English cases was that of Margaret Neffeld of York who, in 1395, brought witnesses before an ecclesiastical court to testify that she had been attacked by her husband who had wielded a dagger, wounded her and broken her bones (Baur and Ritt, 1983; Freeman, 1979). Despite such evidence, the court held that the case for the then equivalent of a modern-day judicial separation had not been made out and the woman was compelled to continue to live with her husband. The Dobashes (1981), who have conducted one of the few recent examinations of the socio-historical roots of domestic violence, also maintain that for centuries husbands have used violence, both systematically and severely, to dominate, punish and control their wives simply as a husband''s prerogative. They trace community attempts to control such behaviour back to the 15th century when public shaming and ridicule were commonly used by local people to change the behaviour of offending members of their community. They note, however, that such measures were rarely exercised in relation to powerful members of the community. Moreover, community reaction in this respect was reserved only for cases of savage and severe treatment: lesser forms of violence were acceptable and condoned.

A husband's rights over his wife were clearly articulated in English common law. These rights extended to complete control of her property and over her daily affairs. They also extended to having the right to correct and chastise his wife: a husband was allowed to "give his wife a severe beating with whips and clubs...." for some "offences" (Hecker, 1910). The same author contended that it was a right practised by most men regardless of social class. It was thus acceptable, both

3

legally and socially, for husbands to use physical force against their wives: only when this force was used to excess was such behaviour proscribed. The wife, however, had no right to beat her husband. Such rights were based on the notion of the unity of the spouses whereby, as Blackstone (1765, reprinted 1966) phrased it, the husband and wife were "one person in the law" thus requiring the "suspension; of the wife's legal existence. It is not entirely clear how reasonable chastisement and excess were distinguished. The popular maxim that the husband could beat his wife with a rod no thicker than his thumb (which is said to have given rise to the term "rule of thumb") appears to have little or no legal corroboration (Baur and Ritt, 1983, quoting Irving Browne's "Wife-Beating and Imprisonment", *Law Times*, 91, September 5, 1891, p. 322). Blackstone believed that the right to beat one's wife was obsolete but claimed that "the lower rank of people" still clung "to their ancient privilege and courts of law still permit a husband to restrain a wife of her liberty in any gross misbehaviour". Despite Blackstone's pronouncements on its obsolescence, some seventy five years later the legality of the privilege was still being upheld as a general right and it was not until 1891 that the right was finally abolished (Freeman, 1979).[1]

In the latter half of the 19th century, pressure to reform the law gathered momentum. Influential and socially prominent women such as Caroline Norton and Frances Power Cobbe were much to the fore in the movement for reform, though John Stuart Mill, too, added his voice to the debates. During the 1870s considerable concern was generated about the prevalence of violence, especially that of men against wives, in such areas as Liverpool's so-called "Kicking District" (McGregor, 1957). Frances Power Cobbe (1878) systematically collected evidence of that abuse and presented it in her pamphlet *Wife Torture in England*. Although she delineated four main incitements to violence—alcohol, prostitution, heteropathy (that is the converse of sympathy and comprises both anger and cruelty) and squalid living conditions—she saw the cause of such violence as the inequality of the sexes:

> The notion that a man's wife is his PROPERTY, in the sense in which a horse is his property... is the fatal root of incalculable evil and misery. [emphasis in the original]

She did not see the solution as being more severe punishment; instead, she argued for separation orders to be issued by the magistrates' courts. Success was to come: this was achieved in the *Matrimonial Causes Act* which was passed in 1878. This gave magistrates the power to grant a separation order with maintenance to a wife whose husband had been convicted of aggravated assault if her future safety was in peril. That proviso was removed in 1895.

---

[1] Freeman, however, also records that judges have more recently defended the right of a husband to correct his wife: in 1946 (though this judgement was reversed by the Court of Appeal); in 1959 when the judge stated that it would not have been cruel to punish a wife as "one punishes a naughty child"; and again in 1976 when a Scottish judge expressed the view that "reasonable chastisement should be the duty of every husband if his wife misbehaves", qualifying precisely that "it is a well-known fact that you can strike your wife's bottom if you wish, but you must not strike her on the face". It should not be thought that these were peculiarities of English (and Scottish) law. Jolin (1983), for example, claims that as recently as 1976 a Pennsylvania town ordinance sanctioned a husband's violence against his wife provided he did not act in such a manner after 10 o'clock in the evening or on Sundays.

Although prior to the First World War, both the British and American suffragist movements embraced domestic violence within their concerns, it virtually disappeared from the agenda of 'social' problems between 1920 and 1970—a fact which Freeman (1979), Borkowski *et al*. (1983) and Wilson (1983) attribute to the absence of a strong Women's Movement. During the 1970s the problem of domestic violence once again generated considerable interest. The influential role of the publicity given to Erin Pizzey's early work in setting up a refuge for women in Chiswick (see Pizzey, 1974) is acknowledged by Freeman (1979), Borkowski *et al*. (1983) and Wilson (1983) but these writers explain that influence as due to the 'sensitizing influence of', or 'the softening up by' the Women's Movement. Certainly, the combination was influential in the establishment in 1974 of the House of Commons Select Committee on Violence in Marriage (hereinafter referred to as the Select Committee). By 1974 domestic violence was also a considerably more visible social problem. By the early 1970s a network of refuges, of which women immediately began to make use, had been established and from which the Women's Aid Federation was to grow. Their existence helped arouse concern and provided demonstrable evidence of a potentially considerable problem.

The establishment of the Select Committee was followed fairly shortly afterwards by the passing of three important pieces of legislation — of which more will be said later in this review—the *Domestic Violence and Matrimonial Proceedings Act 1976,* the *Housing (Homeless Persons) Act 1977* and the *Domestic Proceedings and Magistrates Courts Act 1978*. Thereafter, the problem did not again become the subject of governmental scrutiny until the Women's National Commission, an advisory group to the government, considered it within the more general context of violence again women. Their report (1985) called for, among other things: better police training; more effective inter-agency liaison, including liaison with Women's Aid; greater use by judges of the attachment of the powers of arrest to injunctions made under the *Domestic Violence and Matrimonial Proceedings Act 1976* and the *Domestic Proceedings and Magistrates Courts Act 1978;* extending the period for which injunctions are in force; the maintenance of adequate funding for refuges; and the need for local authorities to be reminded of their responsibilities to give special attention to the housing needs of women who have been victims of domestic violence. Towards the end of 1986 the Home Office, in response to the report of the Women's National Commission, issued a circular (69/1986) to all Chief Officers of Police in England and Wales which stated that the overriding concern in dealing with domestic violence was to ensure the safety of victims and to reduce the risk of further violence. The circular also suggested that Chief Officers might consider how best to ensure that victims could be informed of the sources of assistance available to them.

3 The extent of domestic violence

Problems in estimating the extent of domestic violence

In 1975 the Select Committee concluded that "despite our efforts we are unable to give any estimates of what the likely numbers are". It is still true today that the extent of domestic violence is unknown and that whatever conclusions are reached from the studies which have been undertaken must remain tentative and must be treated with caution. Edwards (1986a) has described domestic violence as the biggest blind spot in official statistics. By its intrinsic nature, domestic violence is an elusive research topic: it takes place behind closed doors; is concealed from the public eye; and is often unknown to anyone outside the immediate family. Even in those cases which do come to the attention of various agencies, their response, as will be discussed later, does not necessarily aid attempts to estimate the extent of the problem. It is not solely the victims and aggressors who often wish to keep domestic violence 'in the family': many others share this attitude. There is general agreement that all sources of information are likely to be under-estimates. Indeed, the 'dark figure' of domestic violence may be greater than that of other crime (Dobash and Dobash, 1979; Hanmer and Stanko, 1985; Worrall and Pease, 1986). The FBI, for example, believes that in the United States domestic violence is the most unreported crime and estimates that it is probably ten times more unreported than rape (Durbin, 1974). This continuing absence of authoritative statistics is thought to limit the ability to take preventive or remedial action (London Strategic Policy Unit, 1986).

There is no single source of information which can be used to estimate the extent of domestic violence. Instead, a composite picture has to be built up from a variety of sources. For example, information cannot be readily obtained from the published *Criminal Statistics* since they do not separately distinguish this form of violence as a category of offence. Instead, the information, based on official criminal records, which is available is the product of specific research studies. Additional information is also available from diverse sources: the statistics of civil court proceedings; national crime surveys; surveys of the general population on domestic violence; surveys of special populations such as students or refuge residents; surveys of different 'agencies', for example, social work departments, hospital casualty departments, GPs' surgeries and so on. All pose problems both individually and collectively.

Before considering the difficulties associated with individual sources of information, however, there are fundamental points which need to be considered

6

in any discussion of the extent of domestic violence. There is firstly the question of how 'extent' is to be measured. Distinctions need to be drawn between measurements of incidence as opposed to prevalence. Moreover, estimates of the number of relationships affected by domestic violence — whether per year or ever so affected — tell us nothing about the frequency with which violent acts occur within those relationships — whether it is once, several or numerous times. There are also problems of exactly what is being measured; for example, what definition of violence is used as the basis for the measurement? Sometimes in the research this is restricted to purely physical abuse resulting in bodily harm — with distinctions often being drawn between levels of severity of injury — whereas, on other occasions, violence is defined as incorporating both physical and psychological abuse and sometimes sexual abuse. Problems of definition also arise in respect of which relationships are defined as 'domestic'. Sometimes this is restricted to legally married couples living together but other research studies include co-habiting couples within their definitions and some include separated or divorced couples. The definition of domestic relationships has also on occasions been extended to include both homosexual and 'dating' relationships. The task of building up a picture of the extent of domestic violence from the various sources of information is thus complicated by problems of definition, operationalisation and measurement.

Individually, each source also has its own limitations. For example, the statistics which appear in *Criminal Statistics* are affected by both public reporting habits and police recording practices. There are many reasons why people do not report crimes to the police (see Hough and Mayhew, 1983; 1985). Included among those reasons are that they may regard the matter as too trivial, or something the police would not be able to do anything about, or they may not define what has happened as a crime. In recording offences, police officers have to be satisfied that the incidents reported to them do in fact meet the legal criteria of what constitutes an offence. Their judgement is obviously bound to a large extent by the criminal law, police procedures and evidential requirements but the exercise of any judgement is also influenced by subjective interpretation of what has happened.

It is thought that domestic violence is a crime only rarely reported to the police but there is no agreement as to what proportion is so reported. The Dobashes (1979), for example, suggest 2%; Walker (1979) suggests 10%; Pahl (1985) estimates that it is 71%. There are other widely varying estimates. The highest rates of reporting to the police are shown in studies — such as Pahl's (1985) — of women living in refuges. This is not surprising since many of the women who seek such shelters have already tried other avenues of help. In a survey into experiences of domestic violence conducted by *Woman* magazine in 1985, one in four women who reported experience of such violence had told no one about their experience and, of those who had, only 28% had gone to the police. This compares with 75% who sought help from relatives; 59% from friends and 39% from doctors and/or solicitors (multiple responses were allowed) (London Strategic Policy Unit, 1986). What proportion of reported domestic violence is in fact recorded by the police? Again,

7

estimates vary but the proportion seems low. Edwards (1986 b and d), for example, found in her study of two London boroughs that only about 12% of all reported cases of domestic violence were made the subject of a crime report by the police and, of these, more than four fifths were later 'no-crimed' ie not officially recorded as a crime.

There are other difficulties in trying to obtain a picture of the level of domestic violence from records compiled by the police for, as was stated above, this is not a specific category of offence and there are no separate records kept in any easily retrievable form. Domestic assaults are, theoretically, treated in the same manner as assaults between strangers. There are four principal types of assault defined by the *Offences Against the Person Act 1861:* common assault (s. 42); actual bodily harm (s. 47); malicious wounding (s. 20); and grievous bodily harm (s. 18). Of these, common assault is not an arrestable offence and is not included in the statistical returns of offences made to the Home Office. With the exception of homicide, official *Criminal Statistics* do not provide information on the sex of the victim nor is the relationship between offender and victim routinely recorded by the police or presented in *Criminal Statistics*.

Victim surveys, though not without their limitations, are in general a good vehicle for overcoming some of the problems associated with criminal statistics. Experience has shown, however, that they are not so effective in measuring offences such as rape and domestic violence. Women are reluctant to admit to being victims of such offences. The reasons which stop them reporting to the police also operate in crime survey interviews. Stanko (1985) explains why women's experiences do not show up in crime surveys as being a result of their growing up in a male-dominated world in which they learn that women's definitions, perceptions and assessments are at odds with men's and that it is the latter that 'count' in public assessments. She argues that women have learned to define their worlds and their experiences as less important than men's. The prevailing notion that "only 'bad' girls get hurt" means that "rather than being exposed as 'bad', women stay quiet". Hough and Mayhew (1983), more prosaically, note that non-reporting may be a result of "their assailant [being] in the same room at the time of the interview."

Finally, individual research studies are bedevilled by the difficulties of generalising from their findings to the general population. There have been only two major national studies, both conducted in the United States, drawing on representative probability samples (Straus, Gelles and Steinmetz, 1980; Straus and Gelles, 1986). Most research studies have relied on small samples drawn from special populations. A common method has been to survey residents of women's refuges (see, for example, Gayford, 1975; Pahl, 1985). These may represent only the more extreme cases. They are probably biased also towards working class women who have fewer resources and greater need to rely upon shelters or refuges than middle class women. Moreover, the focus of attention has been on the victims: little is known about their abusers except for the information provided by their victims.

Court statistics on divorce petitions and proceedings in county courts and magistrates' courts, under the *Domestic Violence and Matrimonial Proceedings Act 1976* and the *Domestic Proceedings and Magistrates' Courts Act 1978* respectively, for family protection or exclusion orders also can shed some light on domestic violence. Their main drawback, however, is that these sources deal only with marriages which are 'in trouble': they provide little insight into how pervasive violence or the threat of violence is within 'functioning' or ongoing relationships.

Information from studies of homicide

Criminological studies of homicide have revealed important information on the extent to which these offences are of a domestic nature. The Dobashes (1979), for example, in their historical examination of domestic violence, discovered that an analysis of homicides in England and Wales between 1885 and 1905 had shown that over half of all murder victims were women with long-standing relationships with their murderers. Out of a total of 487 murders committed by men, just over a quarter were murders of their wives whilst a further quarter were murders of lovers and sweethearts. More recently, the studies of homicide conducted by Gibson and Klein (1969) between 1957-1968 have shown that of all female victims, wives and cohabitants comprised the largest category of victims. Gibson (1975) concluded that women were much less likely to commit homicide than men and that most women victims were closely associated with the murder suspect. Homicide statistics for England and Wales for the period 1972-1982 showed that between 21% and 29% of all victims were acquainted with their killer as spouse, cohabitant, lover or former lover. A special analysis in 1982 showed that a quarter of homicides were domestic. In 2% of the homicides, husbands were killed by their wives; in 18%, wives were killed by their husbands (Edwards, 1986b).

In the United States, Wolfgang (1958) found that 41% of female murder victims were murdered by their husbands whereas only 10% of all male murder victims were killed by their wives. Primary contacts (that is "relatively close, intimate, personal and direct [relationships]") accounted for almost two thirds of all victim-offender relationships. In an examination of the degree of violence used, Wolfgang concluded that the home was the most frequent setting for severe violence: the most brutal murders were committed there and wives were much more likely than husbands to be the victims of such brutal murders. Walker (1978) claimed that the FBI estimates that just over a half of all murders of women are committed by men with whom they have intimate relationships. In 1984, FBI statistics showed that one in three female homicide victims died at the hands of a husband or partner (Herrington, 1986).

Information from studies of assaults

Similar patterns are revealed in relation to assault. McClintock (1963) found that almost a third of all violent offences occurred within the home and Gibson and

DOMESTIC VIOLENCE

Klein (1969) estimated that as many as 90% of all violent incidents occurring within the home were incidents of men assaulting women. The Dobashes' (1979) examination of 3,020 cases of violence reported to the police in Edinburgh and Glasgow revealed that over one third of those cases involved family members and that three quarters of those were wife assault. (By contrast, only 13% of non-family violence was committed by men against women.) There were only 12 reports of wives assaulting husbands (1%) and 6 reports of assault in which husbands and wives were both victims and aggressors.

In evidence given to the Select Committee, the Metropolitan Police, on the basis of a study (the details of which are not given) conducted in 10 police stations over a three month period in 1974, estimated that there were just over 6,000 cases of domestic violence reported to the police per year in the Metropolitan Police District. However, a more recent study by Edwards (1986b) puts the figure much higher. She examined *all* police records — from station message books to crime report forms — in two police divisions — Holloway and Hounslow — over a six month period. From this basis, she estimated that over the whole Metropolitan Police District there were just under 60,000 *reported* incidents per year of which only about 7,000 would be *recorded* by the police as assaults.

Information from population samples

(a) Crime surveys

It has already been said that crime surveys have not been as successful in estimating levels of domestic violence (or rape and other sexual assaults) as they have other forms of crime. The British Crime Survey, for example, (Hough and Mayhew, 1983) in its 1982 'sweep' found that 10% of assault victims were women who had been attacked by present or previous husbands or boyfriends and identified only one rape (attempted). In the 1984 'sweep', Hough and Mayhew (1985) estimated that one in eight incidents of assault and crimes of violence involved family, lovers or ex-lovers. This would amount to just over 200,000 incidents of domestic assault uncovered by the British Crime Survey for England and Wales in 1983. Hough and Mayhew (1985), however, think that this figure is an under-estimate. A re-analysis of BCS data was carried out by Worral and Pease (1986) of all crimes (and attempted crimes) involving contact, including assaults of the person, sexual offences and robbery, in which the offender was seen by the victim and could identify whether or not they knew the offender. This examination does not yield direct information about domestic violence *per se,* only about offences which *may* include domestic violence. Nevertheless, they found that female victims were much more likely to say that they knew the offender well and, in almost two fifths of the cases with female victims, the offender was a spouse.

Other crime surveys claim, however, to reveal a higher incidence of domestic violence. The Islington Crime Survey (Jones, MacLean and Young, 1986) estimated an annual total of 2,500 incidents of domestic violence — about a quarter of all assaults — in the borough. The London Strategic Policy Unit (1986) has extrapolated from these figures and has suggested that this could mean a figure for London as a whole of over three quarters of a million.

In the United States, evidence from the National Crime Surveys from 1978 to 1982 found that an estimated 2.1 million women were victims of domestic violence — defined to include rape, robbery, aggravated or simple assault—*at least once* during an average 12 month period. Moreover, an estimated one third were victimised *again* during the 6 months following their 'initial' victimisation. By contrast, only 13% of the victims of stranger-to-stranger crimes were subsequently victimised by strangers during the six month follow up period (Langan and Innes, 1986).

(b) Other surveys

There has been no large national study in this country specifically concerned with investigating domestic violence in the general population by means of a representative sample. The work of Straus, Gelles and Steinmetz (1980) in the United States is thus particularly instructive. This exploded the myth that domestic violence is a rare and inconsequential occurrence. The survey was conducted in 1975 and involved a representative sample of 2,143 married couples. The definition of violence used was "an act carried out with the intention of, or a perceived intention of, physically injuring another person". They found that one in every six couples had engaged in violent acts against the other in the previous year and that over a quarter had done so at some point during the marriage. Straus, Gelles and Steinmetz (1978) argue that this is very likely a substantial under-estimate. They assert, on the basis of their pilot studies, that:

. . . the true rate is closer to 50 or 60 per cent of all couples than it is to the 28 per cent who were willing to describe violent acts to our interviewers.

Straus, Gelles and Steinmetz (1980) distinguished between "ordinary" or "normal" (*sic*) violence within the family and "severe" or "abusive violence". "Ordinary" or "normal" violence was defined as "throwing things, pushing, grabbing and slapping". Their analysis showed that almost 7% of couples had "thrown something" at a spouse in the previous year and that 16% had done so at some point in the marriage. The statistics for "slapping" were very much the same as for "throwing things". The figures for "pushing, shoving and grabbing" — the highest in the survey — revealed that 13% had done so in the previous year whilst one in four had done so at some point in the marriage. "Severe" or "abusive" violence was defined to include "punching, biting, kicking, hitting with an object, beating-up, threatening or using a knife or gun". This measure revealed 6% of couples had been affected by serious domestic violence in the previous year and almost 13% at some point in their marriage. Looking only at the *most* serious of the serious incidents — "beating-up"[1] and involving the use of a weapon —

---

[1] A "beating-up" incident *excludes* single incidents of kicking, biting, punching or throwing objects. Its definition lacks clarity. Straus, Gelles and Steinmetz (1980) say that it comes after kicking etc. and before the use of guns and knives. It is, therefore, "more than just a single blow".

between one and two per cent of couples had experienced a 'beating-up' in the previous year; one in 20 couples had at some point in their marriage; one out of every 200 couples had used a knife or gun in the previous year, one out of 27 couples had used such a weapon at some point in the marriage. Straus, Gelles and Steinmetz (1980), therefore, estimated on the basis of these figures that at some point in the marriage over 1.7 million Americans had faced a husband or wife wielding a gun or knife and that over two million had been involved in what they term a "beating-up" incident. If all the acts they include in their definitions of "serious" or "abusive" violence—not just "beating-up" or "involving the use of a weapon"—were considered the figure is higher: almost 3 million.

Husbands were only slightly more likely to use violence against wives than *vice versa*—12.1% of husbands and 11.6% of wives had committed acts of violence in the previous year on the other spouse. This finding has generated considerable controversy since it is out of line with many other studies. Even Straus (1980d) admits that it is ". . . inconsistent . . . with my own impression based on a qualitative assessment of interviews with violent couples . . .". In particular, it has been criticised for failing to distinguish between offensive and defensive violence and for ignoring the differences in strength and fighting skills between men and women (Russell, 1982; Gelles and Cornell, 1985; Pagelow, 1985). Straus (1980d), however, conducted additional analysis of the data and concluded that the average number of *severe* assaults by husbands on non-violent wives was three times greater than the number of severe violent assaults on non-violent husbands and concluded that "husbands give more than they receive in the way of violence". Moreover, Straus was of the view that women did not resort to severe violence until they had been the victims of a virtually continuous stream of minor violence by husbands. Although the question of defensive violence by wives could not be addressed directly, Straus thought that the indirect evidence was such as to suggest that a substantial part of the violence by wives was in self-defence.

A replication study ten years later again found high rates of spousal violence (Straus and Gelles, 1986). Nevertheless, the rates had dropped (although not statistically significantly so) in the intervening periods: wife abuse, for example, was 27% lower in 1985 although Straus and Gelles draw attention to the fact that despite such a drop, their findings provide an estimate of 1.6 million wives who were the victims of all types of violence included in the Straus, Gelles and Steinmetz scale of "serious" or "abusive" violence. This replication also confirmed the findings of the earlier study that women were about as violent as men. Straus and Gelles (1986) stress, however, that it is all too easy to misunderstand both the meaning and consequences of that violence, for the reasons outlined above.

Other studies, based on non-random samples of the population, have included samples of students and volunteers. Straus (1974) asked first year sociology and anthropology students at the University of New Hampshire about conflict in their families during their last year at school. 16% of their parents were reported to have used physical force. Gelles (1974) undertook one of the first volunteer studies of domestic violence. He interviewed 80 families in two New Hampshire towns: half the families were known to either the police or social agencies as having a violent history, the other half had no such known history and, therefore, acted as the control group. He found that almost two fifths of his control group reported at least one incidence of violence between husband and wife and that violence was reported as a regular occurrence in over a tenth of the control families.

There have been few surveys in this country which shed light upon the extent of domestic violence. Hanmer and Saunders' (1983; 1984) study in a Yorkshire community focussed on women's experience of male violence and showed that, of the 129 women interviewed, three fifths reported some form of "threatening, violent or sexually harassing behaviour" toward them in the past year. Moreover, about a fifth of these had occurred within their own homes.

Another recent study by Andrews (1987) is interesting in that it did not set out to examine domestic violence but rather the social origins of depression in women. The study was based on a random sample of 400 working class women in Islington. Experience of domestic violence was mentioned so frequently by these women that Andrews decided to investigate it more thoroughly in the third wave of her study which comprised 286 women. One woman in four reported having been involved in domestic violence at some time in their lives. Only 14% of those reported having hit their husbands and all but one of those reported that they had hit back in self-defence.

Information from civil court statistics

Violence is often cited as a cause of marital unhappiness in divorce proceedings. An early study by Chester and Streather (1972) of over 1,500 divorce cases in a large English city during the years 1966-68 revealed that physical abuse by the husband was the most frequently cited reason for seeking divorce. Over 90% of the women mentioned physical abuse as at least one of the reasons for divorce and the majority of these women indicated that violence was a recurring aspect of the relationship.

Elston, Fuller and Murch (1976) estimated that more than two thirds of "English wives petitioning for divorce each year . . . suffer from serious brutality". Parker (1985) has shown that in 1980, over 150,000 divorce proceedings were granted, 70% of the petitioners being women. The most popular ground for divorce was unreasonable behaviour which accounted for one third of all divorces and women were the petitioners in 89% of these cases. In practice, Parker states, the majority of such petitions include allegations of violence and they usually succeed if there is corroboration of some of the incidents and at least one of them was within six months of the couple's separation. Even on the basis of this limited definition, these data suggest that, in 1980, as many as 45,000 marriages in England and Wales were ended as a result of violence by husbands against their wives.

Research in the United States also gives an indication of the extent to which violence figures in divorce. O'Brien's (1971) study of "divorce-prone" couples in

13

a midwestern town revealed that 28 of the 150 individuals interviewed spontaneously mentioned violence — the majority of these reports of violence came from women. Levinger's (1966) study of 600 couples applying for divorce in Ohio showed that wives complained eleven times more frequently than husbands about physical abuse. A more recent study in Northern Ireland found that among nearly 300 divorced and separated women, over one half had been victims of domestic violence (Evason, 1982).

Finally, some indication of the extent of domestic violence — albeit limited since these figures reflect the number who are prepared to go to court — can be gained from the *Statistics of Domestic Proceedings in Magistrates' Courts* and from *Judicial Statistics*. In 1987 (Home Office Statistical Bulletin, 20/1988) about 6,000 applications were made under the *Domestic Proceedings and Magistrates' Courts Act 1987* by which magistrates were empowered to make orders for the protection of a party to a marriage or to a child of the family. This number was 600 fewer than in the previous year continuing the decline from the peak of 8,700 in 1984. Approximately half the general applications were granted (only 5% were refused; the remainder were withdrawn) and 94% of the applications for "expedited orders" (that is where there is imminent danger to the applicant or a child) were also granted. In about one third of the general applications and in about one half of the applications for expedited orders a power of arrest was granted enabling a constable to arrest, without warrant, a person suspected of breaching the protection or exclusion order. In 1987, excluding injunctions made during the course of matrimonial proceedings, about 16,500 applications (including 463 applications to the Principal Registry of the Family Division) were made to the County Court under the *Domestic Violence and Matrimonial Proceedings Act 1976 (Judicial Statistics, 1987)*. This was just over 400 more than in 1986 and almost 3,000 more than in 1985. Of the applications in 1987, only 3% were refused. Almost 70% of the injunctions in 1987 were against non-molestation. Almost three tenths of all injunctions granted had powers of arrest attached. These statistics do not provide a breakdown by the sex of the applicant.

Various researchers have tried to suggest figures of the extent of domestic violence in this country. Freeman (1979) — extrapolatating from the Straus, Gelles and Steinmetz (1980) data for the United States — has estimated that there are around half a million married women who are the victims of domestic violence each year in England and Wales. Marsden and Owen (1975) estimated that serious violence could occur in as many as 1 in 100 marriages whilst, in a later work, Marsden (1978) put the figure at 5% of British marriages. On the other hand, Borkowski *et al.* (1983) have suggested that something between one in five and one in three of all marriages experience physical violence at some point. None of these figures, however, can be accepted with any confidence as to their accuracy. The individual and collective problems posed by the various sources of information mean that there is simply no reliable estimate of the extent of domestic violence. Nevertheless, notwithstanding all the problems involved, the composite picture which can be built up suggests that the inescapable conclusion must be that domestic violence constitutes a pervasive problem.

14

4 The nature of the violence

Who are the victims?

It has already been shown that, with the exception of the work of Straus *et al.* (1980), most research testifies to the fact that in the overwhelming majority of cases, domestic violence is perpetrated by men against women. Data from the US National Crime Survey, for example, have shown that 95% of all assaults on spouses or ex-spouses during 1973-77 were committed by men (US Department of Justice, 1983). Statistics tend to show a concentration of domestic violence occurring within working class families. McClintock's (1963) study, for example, showed that working class families accounted for 85% of the 1,527 recorded cases which he identified as family violence. Straus (1977), in the United States, found a consistent tendency for violence to have occurred more frequently in marriages of 'blue collar' as compared to 'white collar' workers. More recently, Gelles and Cornell (1985) found the highest rates of violence among families living in large urban areas with low incomes, where the husband was either a 'blue collar' worker or unemployed.

Pagelow (1981a) has described the view that domestic violence is solely, or in the main, a phenomenon found among the lower classes as a widely held myth. Such a view should certainly be treated with some caution, if not scepticism. It may be, for example, that middle class families are less willing to admit its occurrence, are less willing to draw outsiders' attention to problems they experience and make more use of private medical care and other resources. It has to be borne in mind, too, that much of the research on domestic violence has concentrated on the lower socio-economic groups. Cannings (1984) has suggested that this is, in part, due to financial support being more readily available for studies of "the needy". Researchers, however, have also tended to make use of both police and social welfare records. From a police perspective, the lower classes have greater visibility. The working class wife is, therefore, more likely to come to their attention — indeed, she is more likely to rely on police intervention since she has few other support systems (Pagelow, 1981a). Moreover, she is more likely to come to the attention of social welfare agencies. A great deal of research has also been based on samples of women living in refuges. The need of working class women for such refuges is likely to be greater than that of middle class women who may have access to more resources and a wider range of alternative sources of help — families, for example, with the financial ability to support them for a while or to offer accommodation.

But not all research points to the greater involvement of working class families in domestic violence. Pagelow (1981) reviews a number of studies which have shown high rates of violence in affluent middle class communities. This leads her to conclude that "wife battering crosses socio-economic lines". She did, however, discern differences in the style and type of violence experienced: middle-class male abusers were much more likely than their working class counterparts to take care that the violence they inflicted was more covert and less visible; they used techniques which rendered no easily visible bruises and they rarely hit their wives' faces. They were also more inclined to use psychological violence. The US Attorney General's Task Force on Violence in the Family (1984) also received evidence of serious abuse endured by professional people. In this country, Andrews (1987) found that although her original sample of 400 women was predominantly working class, one fifth of the sample participating in the domestic violence component were from middle class backgrounds and "many of them still had middle class lifestyles". She found little difference between the classes, noting that "if anything there was a slightly higher rate among those with middle class backgrounds".

The view that domestic violence is the preserve of the working class, therefore, has been attacked by many writers (see also Dobash and Dobash, 1979; Langley and Levy, 1977; Martin, 1976; Pizzey, 1974; Walker, 1978). In fact, Pagelow (1981a) claims that middle class men are more likely to beat their wives than are working class men. In short, we can perhaps conclude with Walker (1978) that:

> . . .Battered women come from all walks of life. Social class, family income, level of education, occupation, and ethnic or racial background make no difference.

and with Goolkasian (1986) who concurs with Walker but reminds us that:

> . . .battering among disadvantaged socio-economic groups is more likely to come to the attention of public agencies.

The scale and severity of violence

Despite disagreement over many aspects of domestic violence by various researchers, one of the few things about which there is almost universal agreement is that it escalates in frequency and intensity over time. Numerous studies have exploded the myth that serious injuries seldom occur or that weapons are seldom used. If violence happens once, it is likely to happen often (Carlson, 1977; Dobash and Dobash, 1984; Dobash et al., 1985; Gelles, 1974; Pahl, 1985). The specific details on the type of violence revealed by numerous studies includes: slaps (backhanded and open handed), shoves, hits, punches, pushes, throwing across the room, throwing down stairs, backing into walls and objects, tripping, kicking, stamping, twisting arms and legs, hitting with objects, choking, biting, burning, stabbing, shooting, throwing out of cars and drowning (Dobash and Dobash, 1981; Martin, 1978; Walker, 1985). To this list of physical abuse some researchers add psychological abuse tantamount to "psychological torture" (Walker, 1985) and others include sexual abuse, including rape[1] (Russell 1982; Walker, 1985;

---

[1] Although the legal systems of some countries recognise marital rape, the law in England and Wales generally does not but there are some exceptions to this general rule. For a discussion see Freeman, 1985.

Wilson, 1983). Frieze's (1983) research, for example, revealed that one third of those women reporting domestic violence had been raped by their partners. Often those rapes, as in Russell's (1982) study, were accompanied by physical beatings. Bowker (1983), too, states that sexual perversion and rape were important components of the violence inflicted on women by their partners. Many women who are victims of domestic violence report that it is a particularly common occurrence during pregnancy (Pagelow, 1981a; Gayford, 1978). Indeed, Andrews (1987) found that many women reported more severe beatings when they were pregnant than at other times and those in her sample who had experienced domestic violence were more than twice as likely as the women with no such experience to have had a miscarriage or stillbirth.

Dobash and Dobash (1979; 1984) constructed a severity of violence scale in order to capture the nature of a typical attack experienced by the women in their study. The scale included specific information about each incident, including information about the type of physical attack (for example, kicking, butting, hitting), the type of injuries inflicted (for example, bruises, burns, fractures) and the number of different types of injuries sustained. Each violent incident was rated on each of these three measures and given an overall score on the severity scale. The distribution of scores was divided into four categories: low, medium, high and extreme. Only a very small proportion were assessed as low in severity, while almost half were assessed as of medium severity and just over half were scored as high or extremely high. The Dobashes, in common with other researchers, found that violence entered the relationship early: half of the women in their sample were assaulted within the first year of marriage or cohabitation and there were very few cases in which the violence emerged after the first three years. They, like Pahl (1985), found that the majority of women had suffered violence for many years prior to finding refuge in a shelter. Moreover, in addition to the number of years during which the violence continued, the frequency increased—in line with the findings of other studies—so that for most of the woman in their sample, this usually meant approximately two attacks per week.

Physical effects

The Dobashes (1984) present both qualitative and quantitative data which demonstrate a broad range in the nature and severity of injuries. The most common form was bruising, often extensive, followed by cuts. In the words of one woman in their sample:

> He knocked me out, my face was bruised and all out of proportion. He bruised my back and spine and I sprained a wrist. My body was all marked by this whipping with a metal spring belt. He pulled half the hair in my head out, my mouth was bleeding and I lost a tooth. I had a black eye and split bleeding lips.

Four fifths of their sample had sought medical help at least once throughout the violent relationship, nearly two fifths had sought medical help on at least five separate occasions.

The evidence they gathered led the Dobashes to conclude:

> Untreated injuries and vicious attacks often result in permanent disfigurement... The women we interviewed... suffered serious woundings, bloodied noses, fractured teeth and bones, concussions, miscarriages and severe internal injuries that often resulted in permanent scars, disfigurement... and persistent poor health.

In the Islington crime survey (Jones *et al.* 1986) almost all women who were the victims of domestic violence had experienced punching or slapping; three fifths had been kicked. In just under a quarter of the incidents reported, weapons had been used, ranging from bottles and glasses to knives, scissors, sticks, clubs and other blunt instruments. Nearly all victims had suffered bruising to the skin or eyes, just under a half experienced cuts and a tenth had their bones broken. Nearly half the women had sought medical advice and a quarter of those had been hospitalised, at least overnight.

This evidence reiterates that given at an earlier date to the Select Committee by one woman in response to the question 'What kind of injuries were inflicted on you?' Her reply:

> I have had ten stitches, three stitches, five stitches, seven stitches where he cut me. I have had a knife stuck through my stomach; I have had a poker put through my face; I have no teeth where he knocked them all out; I have been burnt with red hot pokers. I have had red hot coals slung over me; I have been sprayed with petrol and stood there while he flicked lighted matches at me...

The severity of the injuries sustained is detailed in many studies (see, for instance, the examples provided in Pahl (1985) and Bowker (1983)).

Psychological effects

In addition to the physical injuries sustained, it is common for women to suffer psychological damage. Many report symptoms of stress, such as lack of sleep, weight loss or gain, ulcers, nervousness, irritability and some women even report thoughts of suicide (Stanko, 1985). Gayford (1978) records that suicide attempts were common and often repeated by the women in his sample. Walker (1985) documents incidents of high levels of anxiety, fears and panic attacks, depression and other clinical symptoms including an increased sensitivity to further impending violence. She puts the symptoms of victims on a par with ''terror responses''. Jaffe *et al.* (1986a) have shown that women who were the victims of domestic violence had significantly higher levels of anxiety and depression than a comparable sample of women (matched for family income, length of marriage and number of children) who were not victims of domestic violence. Andrews (1987), too, has demonstrated in this country that women who are the victims of domestic violence are more likely to be depressed than non-victims. Again, she characterises the classic symptoms as weight and sleep disturbances, a sense of hopelessness and lack of concentration. All point to the lack of self-esteem evidenced by victims (see also, for example, Martin, 1978). Andrews (1987), however, although noting that the effects of a violent relationship can be long-lasting, also found that if women left the relationship within one year of the start of violence then there was little difference in measurements of self-esteem between them and women who were not the victims of domestic violence.

Within the literature, there is much discussion of the problem of self-blame. Female victims, it appears, do not necessarily see what happens to them as their abuser's problem: rather they reinterpret events and may believe that they have failed as wives. They may experience feelings of shame and humiliation. Because of this, and fearing most of all that they are ultimately to blame, silence is the response of some women: they tell no-one of the violence which they have suffered. Stanko (1985), however, argues that such silence should not be understood as connoting acceptance, whether tacit or not. Rather she sees silence as "a declaration". "It is a way for the powerless to cope with very real situations". That silence is encouraged by a number of factors, including concern for others (for example, the victim's children), fear, and an immobilising terror.

Walker (1978; 1979; 1984 and 1985) has characterised that immobilising terror as a process of "learned helplessness". Basically it is a summation of women's reactions — or rather lack of reactions — to repeated physical, sexual and psychological abuse. Walker did not coin the phrase: rather she adapted it from Seligman (1975) who had administered electric shocks to dogs in cages at random intervals. The dogs rapidly learned that no matter what response they made, they could not stop the shock. When nothing they could do stopped the shocks, they became passive and submissive. When the shocks stopped, they had lost the will to escape. A commonly asked question about domestic violence is "why don't they leave?" Walker's analogy explains this. She says:

> Once the women are operating from a belief in helplessness, the perception becomes reality and they become passive, submissive, helpless.

It does not matter that the women may not, in fact, be helpless; it is sufficient that they *perceive* of themselves as such. The very fact of being a woman is, it is argued (see, *inter alia*, Stanko, 1985; Walker, 1979; Wilson, 1983), to experience a sense of powerlessness. Gender role training encourages women to be more passive and dependent than men (Radloff and Rae, 1979; Radloff and Cox, 1981). It is a short step from that to helplessness, but Walker (1984) also asserts that such helplessness can develop solely from abusive relationships. She concludes:

> Thus, the interaction of gender socialisation with aggressive and other non-contingent behaviours can produce an expectancy that victimisation is a part of woman's life and the best she can do is to survive with a minimum of harm.

Ferraro and Johnson (1982) argue that victims of domestic violence are only capable of leaving the violent relationship once they are psychologically ready to stop rationalising the violence. In the early stages, rationalisation can take a number of forms: there may be a denial that the violence has occurred; or that injuries have been sustained; or that options other than remaining in the relationship exist. Such processes of rationalisation serve to inhibit a sense of outrage and thus to inhibit efforts to leave. It is only when victims reinterpret the violence as dangerous and unjustified that alternative options are sought. This process may take years but catalysts to that reinterpretation include: increased severity of violence; increased visibility of the violence; external definition of the relationship as being violent; and a change in resources.

Effects on children

Victims of domestic violence report that it is a common occurrence during pregnancy. It follows, therefore, that children may suffer direct physical damage — indeed, miscarriages and still births are common amongst abused women. Pagelow (1981a) takes the view that a combination of pre- and post-natal, emotional and physical abuse suffered by children of women who are domestic violence victims often results in a disproportionately high number of their children experiencing handicaps — physical, mental and emotional. Jaffe *et al.* (1986b) and Wolfe *et al.* (1985) have shown that children with backgrounds of family violence have a significantly higher incidence of behaviour problems and diminished social competency skills than comparable groups of children with no history of family violence problems. Moreover, boys were more affected in these respects than girls. In this country, Moore (1975) reported that social workers considered that four fifths of the children from families with a history of domestic violence were adversely affected by it: such children were described as "jumpy", "anxious" and "nervy". There is some evidence also of a "generational transmission of violence", of which more will be said later in this review.

Children, too, are often burdened with trying to stop the violence. The Dobashes (1984), for example, found that in their analysis of "first, worst, and last attacks", almost one half of the incidents of domestic violence took place in front of observers, three fifths of whom were the couple's children. The children's overwhelming response was some form of passive or active support for their mothers. Often they were too small to do anything other than beseech their fathers to stop, but witnessing such violence also led to their screaming, crying and trying to hide. Guilt feelings are said to be common if they do not come to their mother's aid and they, therefore, often attempt to beat the aggressor or physically come between the couple during the course of the violence (Martin, 1978; Melville, 1978). Gelles (1974) has also noted that witnessing domestic violence between their parents can have the effect of teaching children that violence is a legitimate response to problems. He concludes:

> Not only does the family expose individuals to violence and techniques of violence, the family teaches approval for the use of such violence.

The situational context of violence

The Dobashes (1984), in one of the few studies of the situational context of domestic violence, make the point that there is no precise time at which episodes of domestic violence begin or end: instead they state that they form part of a

20

continuing relationship. There is general agreement that incidents of domestic violence most often occur at home, at night, on weekends and on holidays (Gelles, 1974, 1977; Flynn, 1977; Dobash and Dobash, 1979). Dobash and Dobash (1984) also found that most attacks took place in the living room and hall (more than one half of first, worst and last attacks); much less occurred in bedrooms or kitchens. The specific factors leading to any particular event may, however, occur days, months or even years before the event itself. As is to be expected, most, but perhaps rather more unexpectedly not all, are preceded by an argument concerning a specific complaint or issue. The Dobashes (1984), for example, found that two thirds of all incidents began after some form of argument. However, they commented that more than half of those arguments lasted for five minutes or less; just under a quarter between 6-30 minutes; one tenth from 31-60 minutes; and only a few lasted for as long as 5 hours or carried on sporadically over several days. Resort to violence, therefore, comes quickly. The predominant sources of conflict were found to be: possessiveness and jealousy; demands concerning labour and services; and money. Men were most likely to become violent when the women could be perceived as questioning their authority or challenging the legitimacy of their behaviour.

Over a third of the women in the Dobashes' survey offered no active resistance believing that this would only prolong the attack or increase its severity. Others tried different responses: verbal reasoning; screaming, crying or shouting; escaping; pushing their aggressor away; protecting themselves; and hitting back. Hitting back — tried by only one in ten — however, served to increase the violence being meted out, a fact borne out also by Carlson's (1977) study. Kaufman Kantor and Straus (1987a) also report that active strategies (in which they include hitting back, fleeing the scene, or calling someone for help) were adopted only rarely. It has been noted that almost half of the attacks in the Dobashes' study took place in front of observers, in these cases approximately two fifths tried to intervene in a direct manner to stop it, whilst a further two fifths screamed or cried: 15% did nothing.

Walker (1978; 1985) has suggested that there is a cycle of violence which has three distinct phases varying in both time and intensity both for the same couple and between different couples. She describes the first phase as the "tension building" phase during which minor battering incidents occur which the woman learns to control by various techniques. These basically amount to anticipating her partner's every whim, staying out of his way, blaming herself, openly acknowledging his supremacy over her, and never allowing herself to become, or show, her anger towards her abuser. Such techniques, however, may only serve to delay the second stage: the "acute battering" stage. During this period the woman's anger increases, the batterer recognises that he is out of control but, even so, the violence becomes acute. "She gets the beating whatever her response is" (Walker, 1978). It is the third phase delineated by Walker which has caused most controversy. This, she says, is characterised by extremely loving, kind and contrite behaviour from the abuser who knows that he has gone too far and is trying to make it up. "His behaviour is... typical of a little boy who has done something wrong; that is he

21

confesses... and cries for forgiveness.'' It is during this stage that Walker says the woman's victimisation is complete: if she carries on in the relationship, ''she becomes an accomplice to her own battering''. Not all research, however, supports Walker's thesis of this third loving stage. The Dobashes (1984) and Pahl (1985), for example, cast doubt upon it. The Dobashes in particular, although they think there is weak evidence of apology and the quest for forgiveness after the *first* violent act within a relationship, say that there is almost no empirical evidence that this continues with subsequent acts and that, therefore, it by no means forms a usual part of domestic violence.

5 Explanations of domestic violence

Numerous explanations about the causes of domestic violence have been advanced. None seems all powerful and it is tempting to agree — though for different reasons — with Wilson's (1983) view that "The search for causation . . . becomes, in a sense, a wild-goose chase . . . '' It is probably pointless to try to find one theory of causation of a problem which encompasses so many aspects and, therefore, it is more reasonable to seek a multi-dimensional explanation.

Individual pathology

Much of the early research into the causes of domestic violence focussed on the pathological or deviant aspects of violent individuals and, thus, neglected social, cultural or situational factors. There was as much, if not more, concern with the individual pathology of the victim as there was with the aggressor in many instances. It is axiomatic that such an approach individualises the problem: it treats the behaviour as exceptional and places responsibility for solutions solely with the individuals concerned.

Men who batter have been presented as mentally ill, neurotic or disturbed (Faulk, 1974; Gayford, 1975). Gayford (1975), for example, on the basis of information provided by 100 women who had sought refuge in Chiswick Women's Aid, concluded that men who abused their partners were pathologically jealous, badly brought up, spoiled and indulged as children and incapable of looking after themselves. He also described alcohol and gambling problems as major contributors to domestic violence. Roy (1982) has described wife abusers as suffering from low self-esteem, insecurity, high marital dissatisfaction, high levels of stress and poor communication skills. Men who use violence towards their partners are thought to hold rigid criteria for sex roles tasks (Moore, 1979; Sinclair, 1985), anything 'feminine' being regarded as stigmatising to the male. To Gondolf (1985a), anger is the primary trigger to violence whilst Harris and Bologh (1985) believe that feelings of insecurity about masculinity lead husbands to react violently to their wives in order to pass for 'real men'.

Female victims are also regarded as neurotic or mentally ill (Faulk, 1974; Gayford, 1975, 1976; Marsden and Owen, 1975; Scott, 1974), Snell et al. (1964) have described women who are abused in terms which, as Pagelow (1981a) rightly says, are contradictory: passive, aggressive, indecisive, masculine, domineering, masochistic, frigid, overprotective and emotionally deprived. Such female victims were held to have caused their own victimisation by deviating from the norm of

23

'femininity'. Gayford (1975, 1976), too, suggests that the women in his survey may have provoked the use of violent behaviour towards them. He characterised the victim into derogatory stereotypes: ''Tortured Tina''; ''Fanny the Flirt'' and ''Go-Go Gloria'' — stereotypes which imply that the victim's behaviour not merely contributed to the violence but was the root cause of it. This 'blaming the victim' is very common within the literature. Pence (1985), the Director of the Domestic Abuse Intervention Project in Duluth, Minnesota, has written that 'blaming the victim' serves to obscure the basic problems:

Victim blaming becomes the compromise to radical social restructuring.

She describes 'victim blaming' as the ''solution to the dilemma'' and argues that those who accept such a solution are:

. . . most crucially, rejecting the possibility of blaming, not the victims but themselves.

Storr (1974) wrote that nagging, aggressive women are often unconsciously seeking what they fear most. The notion that women want to be hit was given great prominence — and gained much publicity — by Pizzey and Shapiro (1981; 1982). They speculated that both husbands and wives in domestic assaults are violence-prone and asserted that female victims of domestic violence become addicted to violence: they need to be hurt. If their violent relationship ends, it is argued that the women quickly find themselves other abusive partners. Such a view outraged many of Pizzey's early supporters but was sympathetically received by many psychiatrists and therapists, (Andrews, 1987). Neither Andrews (1987) nor Walker (1979, 1985), however, found evidence in their research to support Pizzey's view; for example, Andrews (1987) found that only 3 of the 59 female victims of domestic violence in her sample had entered into subsequent violent relationships after ending the first.

The empirical studies conducted by Straus (1980a, b and c) and Gelles and Cornell (1985) argue against such an individualistic explanation. Their studies showed that men who hit their wives do not have a particularly high incidence of psychological problems. One of the principal problems of this type of explanation is, as Freeman (1979) has commented, that it seeks ''an exceptionalistic explanation of a universalistic problem''. Although it may be useful in understanding a few specific cases, it cannot provide a broad theory to explain the general phenomenon. Most of the research has been based on small, unrepresentative samples; much of the information has come from victims of domestic violence, including that given about their abusers; there has been little research using control or comparison groups of women who have not been domestic violence victims, or of men who have not abused their wives, or of couples in whose relationships domestic violence has not featured. There is, therefore, no way of knowing whether the characteristics identified are not also commonly observed among those who do not commit or experience acts of domestic violence or, indeed, whether the 'explanations' which are proffered are not merely rationalisations.

Social structural explanations

Those who were dissatisfied with the explanations which focussed on individual factors tended to see domestic violence as being a response to social structural factors: for example, a response to frustration, stress and blocked goals. Sources of stress include economic conditions, bad housing, relative poverty, lack of job opportunities and unfavourable and frustrating work conditions. The work of the Family Violence Research Program at the University of New Hampshire has been particularly influential in focussing attention on the importance of socio-structural factors which are seen to be essentially male dominated (see, for example, Straus, 1980a, b and c; Hotaling, 1980; Steinmetz and Straus, 1974; Gelles, 1983). These researchers argue that role expectations are created and defined by such social structures: for example, men are encouraged to be 'successful', to believe that 'success' is attainable, to believe that hard work and other similar virtues will be rewarded by the attainment of the goals that are set. But structural conditions are such that the means of fulfilling such expectations are not similarly provided. The result is stress and frustration which can then precipitate violence. Not only is this true of roles within wider society but also of roles, obligations and standards which are set for individual family members in which dominance patterns are based on sex and age. Thus men are expected to be the 'breadwinners', the 'head of the household', the 'masters in their homes'. By contrast, women are not expected to be so success-orientated: they are expected to look to men for economic support. The roles ascribed for them are those of being 'good wives and mothers'. Again, there is no automatic provision of the means of fulfilling these standards and men who cannot fulfill the goals that are set — or, at least, cannot cope with that failure — are most susceptible to violent behaviour. Not only are socialisation patterns geared to the teaching and legitimation of traditional sex roles but, it is argued, that they teach children that violence is both normal and acceptable under certain circumstances.

In this school of thought there is an interacting combination of individual, group, social and cultural variables which explains domestic violence; each type of variable on its own offers only a partial explanation. Within the New Hampshire group different researchers have concentrated on or emphasised different factors to varying degrees. Social learning in the family was explored by Steinmetz and Straus (1974). Straus (1980a) examined individual variables such as personal aggressiveness and lack of self control. At a later date (1983), he examined abusers' personal experiences of child abuse. Farrington (1980), on the other hand, has focussed upon the individual stress experienced by family members. Other work has examined sexism in institutional arrangements (Straus, 1980b) and the legitimation of violence as an appropriate response to problem solution as apparently demonstrated by the response — or lack of response — by the police and the courts to the problem (Straus, 1980c). Straus' (1987) most recent analysis of "wife-beating" (conducted not at the individual but at the societal level) found that the greater degree of equality between men and women, the lower the rate of "wife-beating" and the weaker the social bonds, the higher the rate of assaults against wives. Gelles (1983) has explicated a link between different levels of variables. His thesis is that sexual and generational inequality in the family is brought about by the normative power structure in society and reinforced by the lack of social control over family relationships which thus limits the 'costs' of violence to men in relation to its 'rewards'. When these social factors combine with individual motivational factors then, Gelles argues, domestic violence ensues.

If violence is a response to particular structural and situational stimuli, then this would also help explain the apparent concentration of the phenomenon within working class families since they are more likely to suffer stressful conditions such as unemployment and poor housing (these were found, for example, by Marsden and Owen (1975) to be major contributing factors to domestic violence) and budgetary constraints (these were indentified by Colledge and Bartholomew (1980) as contributory factors). Working class families experience structural frustration both more frequently and more acutely, have fewer resources to deal with the frustration and, by this reasoning, are more prone to violence (Gelles and Cornell, 1985).

A recent empirical study by Harris and Bologh (1985) in the United States, however, casts light on how such frustrations can also be experienced by middle class professional workers: the precise experience of frustration may differ but the result is the same — violence against wives. The study was based on a small, non-representative sample of male volunteers in a therapy programme for violent husbands. Its conclusions must, therefore, be regarded as tentative. Of the 34 men studied, 17 were from working class occupations, 13 from middle class, 3 from upper middle class (the law and medicine), and 1 was independently wealthy. A content analysis was carried out of all records and tape recordings made during the therapy. To working class men, it was essential to 'keep their wives in line'. In return for being the primary breadwinner, they expected sovereignty in the home. This meant that they expected their wives to show deference and to cater for their every spoken or unspoken demand and not to challenge their superiority. Demanding such behaviour from their wives within the home helped them to compensate for their low status and low income jobs. Maintaining their supremacy in the home protected their self-worth as a man. Brought up in a society where, the authors contend, feelings of self-worth are determined by the occupational structure, their low status in the occupational structure could be compensated by supremacy at home. By contrast, Harris and Bologh found that white collar workers did not espouse traditional male sex roles and did not expect deference but wanted a more egalitarian relationship. Nevertheless, they were still required to fulfil the role of breadwinner in jobs likely to involve heavy responsibilities, long hours and total commitment. These responsibilities precluded their participating fully in the egalitarian relationship they wanted. They found themselves caught between two ideals. This perceived injustice caused increasing rage and hence violence. Thus, both blue collar and white collar workers were caught in cultural definitions of manhood and the constraints that operate in trying to achieve those culturally defined roles.

As individual explanations blamed first the victim and then the abuser, so the social structural approach indicts society — the structure and norms of society are to blame. What is not adequately explained is why violence is seen as the appropriate response.

Feminist explanations

At the core of feminist explanations is the view that all violence is a reflection of unequal power relationships: domestic violence reflects the unequal power of men and women in society and also, therefore, within their personal relationships. It is a view propounded by sociologists (for example, Dobash and Dobash, 1979; Edwards, 1985b), psychologists (for example, Walker, 1984), lawyers (for example, Freeman, 1979; 1984) and practitioners in the criminal justice system (for example, Pence, 1985) alike.

Dobash and Dobash (1979, 1984) employ the notion of patriarchy to explain women's subordinate status. Patriarchy comprises two elements: the structural — that is those societal institutions which define and maintain women's subordinate position and thus prevent them from influencing or changing the social order — and the ideological — that is the socialisation process which ensures acceptance of that order. Both the Dobashes (1981) historical analysis of legal sources and their empirical 'context specific' study (1979, 1984) demonstrate how husbands have sought and still seek to control their wives by violence.

Pahl (1985) has explicitly pointed out that the "taken-for-granted assumptions" about marriage and the role of the family shape the ways in which the roles of women are defined, the ways in which domestic violence is perceived and thus also agencies' response to domestic violence. The ideology of the family and the privacy accorded the family in our society mean that women are, and are seen to be, subordinate to the men they live with. Men are expected to assume their 'natural' role as the dominant adult within the family. Indeed, Wilson (1983) has argued that domestic violence can be better understood if it is seen as an extreme form of normality — an exaggeration of how society expects men to behave as the authority figure in the family — and both Freeman (1980) and Edwards (1985b) argue that the legal system both reflects and sustains this male supremacy. The pathology is, therefore, moved from that of the individual or even of the individual family to the family structure itself and its unequal power structure. Moreover, the family is seen as a microcosm of an unequal society. Domestic violence thus becomes a symptom of the more general demonstration of male violence, a demonstration of the male ethos and the male domination of women.

A number of writers have drawn attention to the economic dependency of women (see, for example, Chapman and Gates, 1978; Homer *et al.*, 1985;Kalmuss and Straus, 1981; Kaufman Kantor and Straus, 1987a; Martin, 1976; 1978). Pahl's empirical study (1985) attests to the importance of the allocation of the control of money within the household. Although Pahl, herself, did not see this as important when she began her study, the women in her sample drew such consistent attention to it that she systematically investigated it: more than three quarters of the women named money a problem area. Husbands seemed to use the control of money as part of a more general attempt to control and subordinate wives. It appeared to be the key element in a marital relationship in which the husband assumed he would be the dominant partner. This finding is consistent with other studies. The Dobashes (1979) found that the majority of arguments preceding violence focussed on husband's jealousy, differing expectations regarding the wife's domestic duties and the allocation of money. Roy (1977), in her American study, found that the four factors most often leading to violence were, in order of importance, arguments over money, jealousy, sexual problems and alcohol. Evason (1982), too, paid particular attention to financial arrangements within marriage. Her sample compared groups of women who had been victims of domestic violence with those who had not: those who had experienced violence were more likely to have had husbands who kept control over finances and who gave their wives money as and when they thought fit. Non-violent husbands were more likely to have opted for joint management of money. Assumptions and expectations about wives' appropriate behaviour were also identified as important by Evason (1982) and Klein (1982). Evason, for example, found that although there were no differences between her violent and non-violent groups in terms of education, social class, age at marriage or length of courtship prior to marriage, wives who had been abused were particularly likely to have had husbands who favoured a traditional model of marriage in which the husband was 'master in his own home'. Any attempt by wives to assert themselves or question that authority was interpreted as wives 'getting above themselves' and, therefore, they had to be 'put back in their place'.

Morash (1986) has pointed out that socio-structural cultural explanations and feminist explanations are not necessarily antithetical despite their use of different paradigms for theory building. She states that both use eclectic methods, although feminist writers place greater store on historical and anthropological analysis whilst socio-structuralists prefer survey methods and analyses of contemporary social structures. The social structure theorists — epitomised by the New Hampshire researchers — start by constructing a model of inter-related variables (though the precise nature of the inter-relationship is not fully articulated) whereas feminist writers identify the variables only after studying the specific contexts within which the violence occurs. There are thus differences in method and emphasis and the two schools are often critical of one another (for example, feminists' insistence that the neutrality of the terms 'family violence' and 'spouse abuse', used by the New Hampshire group and others, serves to detract attention from the real problem which is violence against women) but there are times when the substance and conclusions of their respective works would argue against seeing these approaches being essentially opposed schools of thought. Straus (1977b), for example, agrees with feminists that:

28

The most fundamental set of factors bringing about wife beating are those connected with the sexist structure of the family and society . . . The cultural norms and values permitting and sometimes encouraging husband-to-wife violence reflect the hierarchical and male-dominant type of society which characterises the Western world.

Moreover, some feminists (for example, Dobash and Dobash, 1979) would not reject the relevance of family history, social stresses, use of alcohol, sexual problems and so on, but argue rather that their explanatory power is not sufficient. Emphasising such factors leaves the question unanswered: why are women most frequently the victim?

If these approaches are correct, then their implication for long-term solutions are indeed profound. But what neither socio-structuralist nor feminist writers do is explain why not everyone abuses or is abused though feminists would argue that this does not affect their thesis: some men may choose not to abuse their power but the power is theirs to choose as they wish. Just as explanations which placed blame on individuals failed to be sufficient, so, too, it can be argued that blaming society is insufficient in itself. A more fully integrated explanation of the apparently high incidence of domestic violence is still required. Each theory as it stands is only partial. There remains a need to link socio-structural and cultural factors with personality development and situational factors. It is difficult not to conclude with Couch (1983) that "Reductionism in either direction, toward individual psychopathology or toward the culture or structure of society, should be avoided."

Contributors to domestic violence

Whilst the above review of explanations of domestic violence has concentrated on more general theories of causation, two specific factors — excessive consumption of alcohol by abusers and 'generational transmission' in families — have so often been put forward as 'causes' of domestic violence that a brief examination of their explanatory power is necessary.

The evidence on alcohol abuse is equivocal. It has been repeatedly associated with domestic violence in a number of studies. For example, Gelles (1974) found drinking accompanied violence in almost one half of the families where assaults had occurred. Moreover, many of the wives in his sample said their husbands only hit them when they were drunk. In Gayford's (1975) study, too, over one half of the women in his sample said their husbands were drunk once a week; almost one half that the violence only occurred when their husbands were drunk. Roy's (1982) large-scale study of 4,000 US couples over a four-year period found just over a third of abusive partners had alcohol problems. In Pahl's (1985) study, over one half of the women said their husbands drank excessively. Just under a third named alcohol as the cause of the most recent act of violence. Other studies, however, (for example, Berk et al. (1980) and Bard and Zacker, 1974) have shown little relationship between alcohol consumption and domestic violence while the Dobash research team found that, although one quarter of their sample said their husbands were often drunk when assaults took place, drinking *per se* was insignificant as a source of conflict in the marriage.

The overall view appears to be that, although a link has often been observed, there is no simple cause and effect relationship (Kaufman Kantor and Straus, 1987b). Excessive alcohol consumption, therefore, should not be seen as a cause of domestic violence but as a condition which co-exists with it. Indeed, the view has been advanced (Kaufman Kantor and Straus, 1987b and Pahl, 1985) that excessive alcohol consumption may be more an excuse for than a cause of the violence. Gelles (1974) goes further:

> Individuals who wish to carry out a violent act become intoxicated *in order to carry out the violent act.* [emphasis in the original]

In short, alcohol provides the 'dutch courage'.

The other popular explanation advanced is that of inter-generational transmission within families which thus establishes 'a cycle of violence'. Basically, the contention is that people who observed violence between their parents or who were themselves victims of family violence in childhood are more likely to become abusers and victims than people who never saw their parents fight or were not abused themselves as children. Such children, it is suggested, are socialised to see violence as a way of life and as a legitimate solution to problems. This legitimacy comes not only from the practice of violence within families, but also through witnessing society's apparent condoning of that violence by the lack of effective response by agencies of both the criminal justice and social welfare systems.

Again, the evidence is equivocal. Although Gelles (1974), Fagan *et al.* (1983) and Pizzey and Shapiro (1981; 1982) have used this idea to explain the behaviour of both the abuser and the abused, others question its applicability to the victims. Roy (1982), for example, found evidence to confirm the experience of the abuser between childhood violence and later adult domestic violence but no evidence of this for the abused. The abusive husband's violent background — but not the female victims' — has also been observed by Kalmuss (1984) and Martin (1976).

The explanatory power of this thesis, therefore, must be seen as only partial. The family may act as a training ground for violence or, at least, form part of that training ground, but if it were both a necessary and sufficient condition then there should be no domestic violence committed by those who neither witnessed nor received such violence as children. That is not the case. Moreover, all those who had such violent childhood experiences should, if the explanation is sufficient, commit acts of domestic violence in adulthood. That, too, is not the case.

The conclusion must be that both excessive use of alcohol and inter-generational transmission may be contributing factors but they should not be mistaken as sole, direct or primary causes of all cases of domestic violence.

6 Legal remedies

It is not intended to review fully the scope of 'black letter law', in particular case law, as it pertains to domestic violence: that would be outwith the remit of this review.[1] Instead, this section focusses primarily on the law in practice and examines how far legal remedies provide a solution to the problems faced by victims of domestic violence and how these remedies are put into operation by the relevant agencies. The main issue is whether there is a gap between the 'law in the books' and the 'law in action'. Nevertheless, a brief summary of the main legal remedies will help illuminate that question. Legal remedies fall into two categories: civil and criminal.

Civil law

Three Acts — the *Domestic Violence and Matrimonial Proceedings Act 1976* (hereinafter referred to as the DVMPA, 1976); the *Domestic Proceedings and Magistrates Courts Act 1978* (the DPMCA, 1978); and the *Housing Act 1985* — comprise the main civil remedies to domestic violence. The Housing Act (1985) incorporates the provisions of the earlier *Housing (Homeless Persons) Act 1977* (the H(HP)A, 1977).

Before the DVMPA, 1976 came into force, injunctions were interlocutory and could be granted only during the course of other legal proceedings. The DVMPA, 1976 removed that requirement. Moreover, couples who were not legally married but who were cohabitants were included within its ambit. A third novel feature of the 1976 Act was that the police could be involved in the enforcement of injunctions where powers of arrest had been attached. (The DVMPA, 1976 did not of course affect the power of the courts to continue to issue interlocutory injunctions.) Under the DVMPA, 1976, county courts were permitted to grant injunctions against molestation; 'ouster' injunctions to exclude a spouse from the matrimonial home; and injunctions to require a spouse to allow the applicant back into the matrimonial home. Powers of arrest could be attached if the judge was satisfied that the respondent had caused actual bodily harm to the applicant or a child of the family and if s/he considered that this was likely to happen again. Where no power of arrest was attached, breaches of injunction could result in imprisonment for contempt of court, but this depended on the applicant bringing the breach to the court's notice.

---

[1] Readers interested in knowing more of the details of the provisions of the various legal measures (and how they have been interpreted by the courts) which seek to regulate and respond to the problem of domestic violence are advised to consult, *inter alia*, Freeman (1979, 1987); Maidment (1978, 1983, 1985); Parker (1985) from whose works much of this chapter is drawn.

The remedies available under the DPMCA, 1978 against domestic violence were modelled to some extent on those available under the DVMPA, 1976. However, there are differences between the remedies available under the two Acts. First, whilst spouses can seek remedies under the 1978 Act against domestic violence, cohabitants cannot. Secondly, the 1978 Act provides remedies only against violence and threats of violence: unlike the 1976 Act, but on the recommendation of the Law Commission, it does not provide remedies against molestation or harassment. Thirdly, whilst under the 1978 Act powers of arrest can be attached to orders preventing the respondent from offering violence to the spouse or any child of the family and to orders preventing the respondent from entering the matrimonial home, they may not be attached to orders requiring the respondent to leave the matrimonial home or to orders preventing the respondent from threatening the applicant or any child of the family, although the applicant may apply for an arrest warrant where s/he believes the respondent has disobeyed any of these latter orders. Fourthly, unlike the 1976 Act, it is not expressly provided in the 1978 Act that where a power of arrest is attached to an order the police, if they use the power, must keep the respondent in custody until s/he is brought before a magistrate; although it is provided that s/he must be brought before a magistrate within 24 hours.

The H(HP)A, 1977 — the provisions of which are now incorporated in the *Housing Act 1985* — gave the victims of domestic violence some rights to local authority housing. The scope of the Act extends beyond domestic violence victims but, nevertheless, they were intended to be included within its ambit when the Act was passed. Thus a person was defined as homeless if, *inter alia*, accommodation was available but occupation of that accommodation would lead to violence, or to threats of violence from some other person living in it and likely to carry out the threats. Pregnant homeless women or homeless persons with dependent children were deemed to have a priority need for accommodation. However, the Act does not cover those who have intentionally made themselves homeless and tests of 'reasonableness' are applied. The Code of Guidance issued with the 1977 H(HP) Act laid down that a battered woman who had fled the marital home should *never* be regarded as having become homeless intentionally because it would clearly not be reasonable for her to remain.

Divorce is an option which is sometimes overlooked in considering the civil legal remedies available to domestic violence victims. Petitions are based on irretrievable breakdown and are established by proving one of the following: adultery; unreasonable behaviour; desertion for two years; separation for two years where the other party consents to the divorce; and separation for five years in which case there need be no consent. 'Unreasonable behaviour' is the most common ground for divorce and, as has been shown, the majority of petitions on this ground include allegations of violence.

Until the passage of the *Matrimonial and Family Proceedings Act, 1984* couples who had been married for less than three years were barred from seeking a divorce unless they sought special leave of a judge to present a divorce petition. This was allowable only where the petitioner was suffering exceptional hardship or the respondent had been exceptionally depraved. The 1984 Act removed the three year discretionary bar to divorce proceedings and replaced it with a one year absolute bar. This could cause severe difficulty to the victim of domestic violence since such violence most commonly occurs early in the marriage (according to Dobash and Dobash (1979) two fifths of victims experienced their first attack within six months of the wedding ceremony). Thus those in this position would have to rely on other remedies. (It is worth noting that Scotland has never had any time bar to divorce.) Divorce courts have the power to grant non-molestation orders, exclusion orders and powers of arrest on the same grounds as are applied under the DVMPA, 1976.

Domestic violence often continues even after divorce and poses certain problems in terms of available legal remedies. If matters ancillary to the divorce — financial arrangements, custody and so forth — have been completed, then the divorce court has technically lost its jurisdiction and cannot grant an injunction. It seems, however, that where the interests of the children of the marriage are affected, courts will intervene (*Stewart v Stewart* 1973, All. E R 313). Maidment (1985) has pointed out that divorced partners without children are not covered by the DVMPA, 1976. Divorced victims and former cohabitants may, however, also make use of the law of torts. The torts of assault and battery are possible methods of obtaining an ancillary injunction against assault or trespass in addition to claims for financial compensation. Since 1962, there has been no reason why a party to a marriage cannot sue the other partner for damages for injuries suffered though, as Freeman (1979) has commented, this power is rarely if ever used in domestic violence cases.

Civil law in practice

It is generally agreed (Maidment, 1985 and Parker, 1985) that the judiciary was initially willing to take a sympathetic view of applications for injunctions under the DVMPA, 1976. Protection or non-molestation, the main purpose of the Act, was held to override any other questions of rights — for example to property — which might arise on a request for an exclusion order. With the passage of time, however, a more restrictive approach appears to have emerged.

Although no time limits are normally attached to molestation orders, a Practice Note (1978 2 All E R 1056) has laid down that, with respect to ouster injunctions, a time limit of three months should normally be attached. This means that unless the person granted the injunction keeps coming back to court for extensions, accommodation problems must be sorted out within those three months. The obvious intention of this time limitation is that injunctions are to be used merely as short-term remedies. There are legal procedures available — under the laws regulating divorce and under the Matrimonial Homes Acts — whereby those who are married can seek permanent orders and this is so whether the property is owned or rented. For the cohabitant, however, there are no such special procedures. Where the house is owned, the cohabitant has to prove a share of it by virtue of financial contributions made to its purchase or, failing that, that the cohabitant

33

has a contractual licence to live in the home until any children are grown up. Where property is rented privately, the evidence of an ouster injunction should be sufficient to obtain an assignment of tenancy (provided there is no inhibitory covenant). Ironically, the tenancy of council rented property, since the passing of the *Housing Act, 1980,* cannot be assigned unless security of tenure has been lost through some other action, for example, non-payment of rent. Where there is security of tenure, the tenant must agree to assignment. The *Housing Act 1980* thus created further difficulties for victims of domestic violence. According to Pearl (1986), it is now customary for local authorities to demand court orders prior to making decisions on rehousing. He argues, therefore, that the effect of the *Housing Act, 1980* has been to remove the power of local authorities to intervene at an early stage in the event of domestic violence occurring between couples who are local authority tenants.

Since 1983, too, the overriding issue of protection in making ouster injunctions has also come under attack in respect of the evidence which is required on which to base the injunction. The 1976 Act does not itself lay down criteria and two distinct approaches to interpretation have developed. The first is primarily concerned with providing accommodation for the children of the relationship and was predominant until the case of *Richards v Richards*[2] in (1984 A.C. 174).

The parent who would have care of any children (in practice, in most cases, the mother) would inevitably be given the right to stay in the home and the injunction would require the other, usually the husband, to leave. (This approach did not preclude the courts being concerned with the question whether it was really necessary for either party to leave and, if so, which, or of balancing the hardship that would be caused to each. But, in the main, the ultimate concern was to protect the welfare of children.) It was this possibility of the mother staying in the home on her children's 'coat tails', as Maidment (1985) puts it, that led to the second approach in interpretation, *viz.* that detailed consideration should be given to the conduct of the spouses. Parker's (1985) view is, that, in practice, the argument becomes one of whether the man's conduct warrants the likely consequences *to him* of being excluded from the home.

The judicial interpretation that injunctions should only be a short-term remedy and hence limited normally to a three month period is reinforced by the same period being attached to powers of arrest (*Practice Notes* 1981 All E R 224). Moreover, the Court of Appeal has ruled (*Lewis v Lewis* 1978 1 All E R 729) that the power of arrest is not to be regarded as a routine remedy but is applicable only in exceptional circumstances. (It will be recalled that the Act lays down that actual bodily harm must already have taken place.) This is contrary to the recommendations of the Select Committee which had argued strongly that injunctions would not be enforced unless the police were given this power.

Although the success rate of applications for injunctions under the DVMPA, 1976 is high, there is considerable variation over the country. Furthermore, there is

---

[2] For a discussion of this important case see Hamilton (1984) and Parkinson (1986).

substantial regional variation in the extent to which powers of arrest are attached to injunctions (London Strategic Policy Unit, 1986). Their effectiveness depends on the police being willing to use these powers in the event of a breach, though they may also have a deterrent effect. Variation between courts is also to be found in respect of the type of evidence required — for example, medical reports, photographs, or witness testimony — and in the form in which such evidence is presented — for example by affidavit or oral evidence. The penalties imposed for breaching an injunction order also differ between courts.

Where an applicant is married there is a choice of legal remedies available in either the county courts or the magistrates' courts. It is sometimes suggested, however, that in practice, solicitors often opt for the county court procedure (London Strategic Policy Unit, 1986). On the face of it this might be thought surprising since magistrates' courts are usually less expensive, nearer, less formal, should provide speedier remedies, and can also grant orders such as maintenance and custody. Both Parker (1985) and the London Strategic Policy Unit (1986) suggest that the choice may reflect greater confidence in county court judges than in magistrates to act against domestic violence. Those authors suggest that magistrates' involvement in criminal cases — which require a higher standard of proof than civil cases — has influenced their attitude to the DPMCA, 1978 and, therefore, that they require more evidence of violence. However, this view must be set against the fact that magistrates refuse only a very small percentage of applications for remedies against domestic violence. In 1987, only 5% of general applications and 2% of applications for expedited orders were so refused (Home Office Statistical Bulletin 20/88). Moreover, Murch et al.'s (1987) study of the overlapping family jurisdiction of magistrates' courts and county courts — which, inter alia examined the factors influencing solicitors' decisions as to which court to use in cases where each offered identical or similar remedies — found that, in general, the magistrates' court was the favoured option in cases of personal protection. This decision turned on the speed with which such cases were heard in the magistrates' court and the minimisation of delays.

Although in theory the *Housing Act 1985* — which incorporates the provisions of the H(HP)A 1977 — requires a local authority to rehouse, as a matter of priority, victims of domestic violence who are pregnant or have a dependant child or are homeless and not intentionally so; it appears that the reality is often different. Differing interpretations of the Act's provisions have led to variation in practice across the country. In Brailey's (1985) study of four Scottish local authority housing departments, the proportion of women whose applications for rehousing were successful varied from just under a fifth to just over a half. Binney et al.'s (1981) study of 656 women living in refuges found that, at the time of first interview, local authorities had refused over two fifths of women's requests for rehousing. The grounds for refusal were numerous. It was sometimes argued, for example, that women living in refuges were not homeless.[3] In some cases women were refused because they did not show visible bruising and, therefore, were judged not be victims of domestic violence. In yet others, leaving home voluntarily as a result of violence was judged to constitute intentional homelessness. Refusals were also made in other cases on the grounds that women without dependent children were not a priority need whilst some women with dependent children were required to produce final custody orders as proof of dependency. Maidment (1985) has argued that the decision in *R v Ealing Borough Council ex p. Sidhu* (1982 80 LGR 534), which ruled that dependence was a matter of fact, and not conditional on a prior court order, means that local authorities' insistence on preconditions such as divorce and injunctions are unlawful. In the Binney *et al.* (1981) study, further difficulties were experienced by women who had sought refuge away from their local area. Local authorities have no duty to rehouse if the applicant has no local connection but has a connection in another area and there is no risk of domestic violence in that area. Women were, therefore, often passed from one area to another, each local authority refusing to accept responsibility. It was also found that, even where women were accepted on to housing waiting lists, they could often spend six months to a year in a refuge waiting for an allocation to be made. Overall, Binney *et al.* (1985) conclude that although H(HP)A 1977 had seemed to promise much, the reality was often far short of the promise. Many of the apparent gains had been transitory and the Act's provisions were frequently not interpreted in the favour of domestic violence victims.

Maidment (1985) has also drawn attention to another difficulty: that of challenging local authorities' decision-making. An application for judicial review in the High Court is the only legal procedure available. This does not constitute an appeal on the merits of the case, but is merely an examination of whether local authorities have correctly interpreted the law and applied correct procedures. Nor does a complaint to the Local Commissioner for Administration provide an opportunity for challenging the merits of a case.

Civil legal remedies are thus extremely complicated. Parker (1985) has deplored their lack of integration and said that they are "unintelligible to most of their users." It seems that it is not the remedies *per se* which are lacking — indeed, Maidment (1985) thinks that the legal system provides all the necessary remedies. Commentators, however, share the view that where the legal system really fails is in the application, operation and interpretation of legislative provisions. Parsloe (1987), for example, in an article entitled '*Battered by men and bruised by the law*' argues that the system of obtaining injunctions seems to be weighted against the woman and designed to be discouraging. Moreover, practitioners who come into contact with victims of domestic violence have also been found to be lacking in the most elementary understanding of legal remedies (Borkowski *et al.*, 1983). Clients in need of legal help are consequently not referred to solicitors. The early promise of the reforms of the 1970s seems not to have been realised in practice: a vast gap appears to exist between the law in theory and the law in practice.

---

[3] A court case in 1982, *R v Ealing Borough Council ex p. Sidhu* 1982 80 LGR 534 has settled that this argument was untenable.

Criminal law

By contrast to civil remedies, the criminal law governing incidents of domestic violence appears comparatively simple. All forms of physical domestic violence and some forms of psychological violence — for example, threats of physical injury — constitute criminal offences. Theoretically, the law governing domestic violence is the same as that governing violence between strangers and is covered by the *Offences Against the Person Act 1861*. This deals with a range of offences from common assault to murder. The four sections most usually applicable to domestic violence are: common assault (s. 42); assault occasioning actual bodily harm (s. 47); malicious wounding (s. 20); and grievous bodily harm (s. 18).

Only common assault is not an arrestable offence. Although the law clearly states the criminal status of such offences, there is no enforceable duty on the police — who until the recent advent of the Crown Prosecution Service had responsibility for prosecutions in England and Wales — to arrest and to prosecute in any particular case. It was police policy that common assaults should be pursued in the magistrates' courts by means of private prosecutions. Private prosecutions require some degree of expertise and perhaps a great deal of courage since they leave the private prosecutor open to further intimidation and, possibly, further violence. Moreover, such prosecutions are likely to entail considerable legal expenses since legal aid is not available for them.

Given the apparent clarity of the criminal law, an examination of its operation in practice is essential to an understanding of why there is considerable dissatisfaction with it. This entails an examination of police responses, prosecution practice, the role of judges and the courts, and sentencing practices. Before doing so, however, it is necessary to note two recent changes which affect the criminal law, changes too recent for research to have examined and about which there can only be speculation as to their likely impact. The first is the Crown Prosecution Service which has been mentioned already and which will be returned to later in considering prosecution practice. The second relates to certain provisions in the *Police and Criminal Evidence Act, 1984* (hereinafter referred to as PACE).

Prior to 1978, victims of domestic violence were both competent and compellable witnesses in law, ie a woman could be made — compelled — to give evidence against her husband. An important House of Lords case in that year, however, (*Hoskyn v Metropolitan Police Commissioner* 1978 2 All E R 136) ruled that a wife should not be "treated as a compellable witness against her husband in a case of violence on her by him". It is likely that this was influential in shaping police policy on prosecutions. Under PACE, however, wives are again to be compellable witnesses (s. 80), as they were in common law. PACE also provides new powers of arrest (s. 25(3)) where there is a need to prevent injury or to protect a child or other vulnerable person from the offender. A Home Office Parliamentary Under Secretary, Douglas Hogg, has advocated the use of this power in domestic violence cases (Hansard 3 November 1986). Taken together, these powers should, it could be argued, lead to increased enforcement of the criminal law. Only the passage of

37

time will tell this. Meanwhile, commentators have speculated that there are unlikely to be any significant major changes (Edwards, 1985a and 1986b; Powell and Magrath, 1985; Sanders, 1987). They note that few prosecutors will take unnecessary risks in compelling a witness likely to appear unwilling or even hostile. It is also noteworthy that cohabitants could always be compellable witnesses, yet the retraction of a complaint in this event still influenced police prosecution practices.

When the Criminal Injuries Compensation Scheme was started, victims of domestic violence — whether married or cohabiting — were not included within its scope unlike divorced and separated women. Since 1979, however, it has been possible to claim financial compensation under the *ex gratia* scheme. Certain conditions are attached to such claims: the injuries are worth more than £550 (as judged by damages in a tort action); the offender must not benefit from the award; and the offender should normally have been prosecuted. Exceptions may be made to the general rule that offenders should be prosecuted where there are practical, technical or "other good reasons" why a prosecution has not been brought but the research literature provides no information as to whether this occurred in respect of domestic violence. There has been a low take-up of the 1979 provision (Wasik, 1983), perhaps chiefly because of the general prosecution requirement. As a result of the *Criminal Justice Act 1988*, the Criminal Justice Compensation Scheme is to be placed on a statutory footing. At the time of writing, this provision has not yet been implemented.

Compensation orders were first introduced by the *Criminal Justice Act 1972* which allowed such orders to be made only in addition to some other sentence passed by the court. Ten years later, the *Criminal Justice Act 1982* empowered courts to make such orders as sentences in their own right. Compensation orders involve the payment of money by the offender to the court which transmits it to the victim. Prior to the *Criminal Justice Act 1988* they could be used for any victim who had suffered personal injury, loss or damage as a result of a criminal offence. Recent research by Newburn (1988) has shown that compensation is awarded only infrequently in cases of assault. Attempts are now being made to remedy this (Home Office Circular 86/1988) and under the *Criminal Justice Act 1988* — which also extends the scope for compensation orders — courts are now required to give reasons for not making such an order where they have the power to do so. It will obviously be some time before it becomes known how the courts will apply their powers in cases of domestic violence which come before them.

7 Police responses to domestic violence

A considerable body of the literature on domestic violence has concentrated upon police responses to the problem. Certainly, the police have received more attention than other agencies of the criminal justice system. That is perhaps not surprising since they are undoubtedly the most visible and, arguably, the most accountable part of that system. There is a sense, too, in which they perform the role of gatekeepers, not solely to the criminal justice system but also to other specialised agencies who might help with the many problems associated with domestic violence (Freeman, 1977; Faragher, 1985). They, therefore, are of considerable potential importance to the domestic violence victim. Although not the sole agency available on a 24 hour basis every day of the week, they are perhaps the most accessible on a comprehensive, geographical basis and one whose accessibility is increased by the emergency 999 telephone system. Not only do they provide the first opportunity of invoking the criminal law but, arguably, they ought to provide access, by means of referral, to other agencies, for example, medical, legal, housing, refuge, social work. Most of the literature is, however, highly critical of police responses. Much of the research is American, but British studies are no less critical.

Edwards (1986d) has delineated three main issues with which research has been concerned. First, it has explored how the police actually deal with incidents of domestic violence, with particular focus on whether or not they arrest offenders. Two methods have been used to examine this question. Some studies have analysed police records and/or carried out observations of police behaviour (see, for example, Faragher, 1985; Parnas, 1967; Oppenlander, 1982; Bell, 1984a and b, 1985; and Edwards, 1986b and d) whilst others have relied upon interviews and questionnaires of female victims of domestic violence (see, for example, Binney *et al.*,1981; Bowker, 1983; Brown, 1984; Pahl, 1982a, 1985; Walker, 1984). The Dobashes (1979) combined both methods in their large-scale Scottish study. Second, research has also examined the attitudes and perceptions of police officers in relation to domestic violence. These have often been inferred from the findings and conclusions of research concerned with the first question, but studies are beginning to appear which are based on interviews with police officers themselves (for example, Edwards, 1986b and d; Homant and Kennedy, 1985). Third, research has focussed on victims' views of the service provided by the police. This issue will be discussed later in this review when victims' satisfaction with all agencies, not just the police, is examined more fully.

Despite their accessibility and the fact that they are regarded as the agency charged with responsibility for protecting the public, individually and collectively, against crime, the police are not the first and major contact for most domestic violence victims. Pahl (1985) found that most women in her sample first sought help from relatives or friends before turning to formal agencies for help. Even then, police help was not the first to be sought. The normal pattern was to contact doctors, social workers or lawyers before turning eventually to the police. (Even then, many domestic violence victims *never* call the police.) Turning to the police for help thus tends to occur only after a sequence of violent attacks has already been endured and usually is resorted to when the violence has escalated in severity. Bowker (1983), for example, found that only about one tenth of the women he studied called the police after the first incident of violence but about a third called for their assistance after the worst violent incident.

A considerable proportion of all requests for assistance to the police involves what they tend to term "domestic disturbances" or "domestic disputes". Evidence to the Select Committee in 1975 showed that about a quarter of all weekend emergency calls in one large English city were concerned with domestic disputes. Earlier work by Punch and Naylor (1973) had revealed that one third of all the telephone calls received by three rural police forces in Southern England concerned "domestic occurrences". More recently Borkowski *et al.* (1983) have suggested a lower figure: 7% of all tasks classed as 'responding to the public' (missing persons, sudden deaths, attending fire and so forth). Research in Hampshire by the Policy Studies Institute (1987) suggested that 'domestic disputes' comprised approximately one tenth of all incidents *attended* by police officers. Research in the United States also bears out the high demand for police services which are to do with domestic violence. Wilt and Bannon (1977) found that domestic violence calls formed the largest single category of calls for assistance. Parnas (1967; 1971) and Scott (1981) concluded that domestic violence calls were more common than calls for all other types of violent crime combined.

Record keeping

Despite this considerable demand on police resources, there is very poor record-keeping. In the collection of statistics, for example, domestic assaults are not recorded separately. There is no system of information retrieval whereby an officer dispatched to an incident can readily ascertain whether there have been previous reports on the individual household, how frequently any previous calls have been made, the nature of any previous violence and whether its severity has been increasing over time. Even where instructions do exist regarding the storage and retrieval of injunctions, often they are not followed (Metropolitan Police Working Party, 1986).

In England and Wales, calls for assistance to local police stations are supposed to be recorded on a station message pad, which should also identify the officer dealing with the case and record the outcome of his intervention. Edwards (1986b) found in her London study that advice is often given over the telephone (with no follow-up action) and, when this is the case, often no record is made of the call in the station message book. (She provides no information, however, as to the frequency of these occurrences.) The role of the dispatcher or radio controller is extremely important as research in the United States has shown. Both La Fave (1969) and Parnas (1971) found that it was common practice in the police forces they studied for calls concerning domestic violence to be 'screened out' by the dispatcher, particularly where it did not appear as if *excessive* violence was likely. This was the official policy of the forces concerned and was resorted to especially at times when demands for assistance were high. The justification was limited police resources and the view that such matters were for the civil not the criminal law. Both Cumming *et al.* (1965) in the United States and Dutton (1977) in Canada found that when a domestic violence victim rang the police for assistance there was only about a 50 per cent chance of getting help other than advice from the dispatcher. It seems, too, from Oppenlander's (1982) study of 596 police investigations of arguments and assaults (drawn from 5,688 observations of patrol officer-citizen encounters in 24 communities in three metropolitan areas in the United States) that the information given by dispatchers to officers in cases they refer for investigation tends to be somewhat scanty. There is little probing for information about the nature and seriousness of the incident and officers are normally told little other than "it's family trouble". To some extent, the lack of information may be inevitable since callers may provide only hurried and incomplete descriptions. Oppenlander, however, concludes that the discrepancy in accuracy of information provided in domestic violence assaults *vis-a-vis* other assaults is such as to suggest that the former are regarded as intrinsically less serious by the dispatcher who, therefore, fails to probe to the same extent as would otherwise be the case.

The under-reporting of domestic violence in the initial stages of record keeping is carried through to the more formal later stages both in this country and in the United States. Consequently, there is a lack of official documentation. Where an incident is investigated by the police but the officer, in the exercise of his discretion, decides that the circumstances do not warrant the completion of a crime report (which forms the basis for the compilation of criminal statistics) it is nevertheless supposed to be general practice for an incident report form to be made out describing what happened and the action taken. Edwards' (1986b and d) study of police dispositions of "domestic incidents" in two London boroughs found that this happened only infrequently. Out of a total of 773 cases reported, 93 were made the subject of a crime report; of the remaining 680, incident reports were completed in only 73 cases, a further 45 were noted in the parade book. Even in those few cases on which a crime report is completed, Edwards' findings show that the majority (83%) are eventually 'no-crimed' ie reclassified as not being a crime. 'No-criming' is of course a common police practice in respect of all types of offence (see Coleman and Bottomley, 1976; and McCabe and Sutcliffe, 1978 for a discussion of the practice). Indeed, non-domestic violence is also frequently no-crimed (Coleman and Bottomley, 1976; Chatterton, 1983). However, the high rates found with respect to domestic violence lead to a tendency to seriously underestimate its extent and, thus, 'no-criming' practices can both distort and

41

mislead. (A discussion of the factors underlying the decision to 'no-crime' domestic violence incidents will be made later in this review.)

Response times to calls for assistance

Another criticism which has been made of police handling of domestic violence relates to the response times of officers in answering calls for assistance deemed by the dispatcher to warrant further investigation. Edwards (1986b) found that, in general, cars would be sent within five to ten minutes but the report by the London Strategic Policy Unit (1986) claims that there were other reports (uncited) of responses taking up to an hour and, indeed, of officers not arriving at all. Certainly, a long response time has also been noted in a number of research studies in the United States and Canada (Berk *et al.* 1980; Bowker, 1983; Dutton, 1977; Loving and Farmer, 1980; Parnas, 1971). Oppenlander (1982), for example, compared response times to domestic violence incidents with those to non-domestic violence and found that, although the travelling time was roughly equal for both, response time took longer for domestic violence and this was despite the fact that they were more frequently dispatched as being 'in progress'. Interviews conducted with police officers during the Oppenlander study revealed that this was a deliberate policy (though not an official policy of the police department) by individual officers who hoped that the extra time would allow the problem to be resolved before they arrived. Again, it seems that patrolling officers share the dispatchers' view that domestic violence should be treated as less serious and less urgent than other reported assaults.

Arrest

It appears that the police both in this country and in North America have traditionally adopted formal non-arrest policies for domestic violence. In evidence to the Select Committee, the Association of Chief Police Officers expressed the view that:

> . . . We are, after all, dealing with persons "bound in marriage", and it is important, for a host of reasons, to maintain the unity of the spouses. Precipitate action by the police could aggravate the position to such an extent as to create a worse situation than the one they were summoned to deal with. The "lesser of two evils" principle is often a good guidance in these situations . . . Every effort should be made to re-unite the family.

Intervention of a more legalistic nature was to be reserved for assaults involving physical injury of a severe nature. Similar policies in the United States have been noted by Bell (1984a and b; 1985), Martin (1978) and Sherman and Berk (1984). Class action suits[1] in both New York and Oakland against the non-intervention

---

[1] This type of legal action whereby one individual can pursue an action, the benefits of which will apply to others in the same position, is not available under English law.

policies of the police won wide publicity and changes are being made, as will be shown later in this review. The critics of non-intervention were aided by research findings of the United States Police Foundation (1976) which showed that in 85 per cent of a sample of spousal homicides, police had intervened at least once in the preceding two years. Moreover, in over half of the homicides, there had been police intervention on at least five or more occasions.

It is not surprising, therefore, that the overwhelming evidence from research is that in cases where officers do intervene in domestic violence incidents, they nevertheless do not arrest the assailant even in cases where there is clear evidence of assault. Surveys of battered women in the United States, for example, by Langley and Levy (1977) report that arrest occurred in only 3% of cases; Roy (1977) put the figure at 10%; and Brown's (1984) study suggests a higher figure of 23%. In Britain, a similar study by Binney *et al.* (1981) showed that the arrest rate was 15% for cases not requiring hospital admission (where severe bruising or black eyes had occurred) and only 20% for cases described by the authors as 'life threatening' ie requiring hospitalisation and including attempted strangulations and drownings. Studies of police records, mostly American, also tend to show low rates of arrest (see Sherman and Berk, 1984 who cite a number of unpublished analyses of police data). Bell (1984b) in his analysis of almost 60,000 domestic dispute incidents reported to Ohio police jurisdictions in one calendar year found that in about two thirds of incidents the police took no action at all; in about one fifth of incidents they made referrals to other agencies; and in only 14% of cases was an arrest made. Black's (1980) observational study in three American cities — Boston, Washington and Chicago — revealed that arrest was a far less frequent response than removing the assailant temporarily from the scene. An observation study, albeit of only 26 domestic violence cases in Staffordshire, by Faragher (1985) also bears out that arrest is used only infrequently. In ten of the 26 cases there had been a clear infringement of the law which could have led to an arrest. Five of these cases involved assaults of sufficient seriousness to warrant a s.47 classification (actual bodily harm). Despite the level of violence involved, an arrest was made in only two, one of which Faragher claims was influenced by his presence. Bedfordshire police (1976), in response to recommendations made by the Select Committee launched a special initiative against domestic violence. Even then, however, arrests were made in only about a third of cases.

It is important to remember, however, that arrest is by no means an automatic response to any criminal offence. Individual officers have considerable discretion in deciding how to deal with incidents. Most of the research on arrest rates discussed above has focussed only on police contacts with domestic violence incidents. An important question is how those arrest rates compare with arrest rates for non-domestic assaults. There have been no British studies which make such a comparison. American research tends to suggest that the police arrest for domestic assault relatively less frequently than for other assault (Bowker, 1982). Black (1971), for example, found that arrests were about half as likely when family members were involved as when strangers were involved. More recently,

43

however, Oppenlander (1982) found the opposite: more suspects were arrested in domestic violence incidents than in other violent cases. This reflected the fact that there were twice as many injured victims in domestic violence than in other types of assaults.

Oppenlander also discovered that charges made against domestic violence suspects were often not assault charges, but were for other offences such as public drunkenness, public nuisance or resisting an officer. In this country, Chatterton (1983), Edwards (1986b) and McCabe and Sutcliffe (1978) also give examples of the use of public order — breach of the peace, drunk and disorderly and so on — charges rather than assault, a point which will be returned to later in this review in considering the prosecution of domestic violence.

It further appears that it is common practice for police to 'downgrade' the injuries sustained. In Edwards' (1986d) study, for example, of the 73 incidents on which an incident report was completed, two thirds were recorded as common assault and the victim advised to privately prosecute despite the fact that in these cases there was visible evidence of assault — bruising, cuts, swelling — and in some a weapon had been used.

There is also evidence that the police do not arrest offenders despite victims' wishes to the contrary. In Bowker's (1982) study, 92% of the women he interviewed (N=146) had asked police to arrest but this happened in only 14% of cases. Pagelow (1981a) provides evidence of victims requesting an arrest to be made only to have the police talk them out of it. Oppenlander (1982) too suggests that what victims want is for officers to enforce the criminal law and not to act as counsellors.

Not only do police officers not arrest for criminal assault: it also appears that the police do not always use their powers when victims of domestic violence have obtained injunctions with a power of arrest. It is, of course, the case that the power of arrest is not mandatory. The London Strategic Policy Unit (1986) claims that the Metropolitan Police are under instructions to arrest only when the police witness the breach of the injunction. Certainly, Edwards (1986b) concluded that arrests were made only rarely. Criticisms have also been made of police administrative systems for dealing with injunctions (Faragher, 1985; the Metropolitan Police Working Party, 1986). It seems that such systems can be inefficient to the extent of officers being unaware of the existence of an injunction and, indeed, of being unable to discover its existence. Even where there is knowledge of an injunction in force, however, the police are often reluctant to enforce the terms of the injunction or to help the individual to enforce it because they view injunctions as the private business of the individual (Faragher, 1985). There is much 'blaming of the victim': the common view is that they invite their abusers back into their homes (Edwards, 1986b).

It also appears from Edwards' (1986b) research that police officers regard injunctions without a power of arrest as 'useless', a 'waste of time', 'not worth the paper they are written on'. Even where there is power of arrest, however, they agree they make little use of it (Edwards, 1986b and d).

The reluctance of police to make arrests has been criticised on a number of grounds. Their lack of action is seen as condoning domestic violence. It fails to afford victims the right to personal protection and may leave them vulnerable to ever increasing attacks. It has been argued that their inaction signals to the aggressor that there is a licence to carry on being violent in the domestic situation. Bell's (1984a) conclusion captures the views of many researchers:

> . . . the police have perpetuated domestic violence by their inappropriate action, as well as their inaction, in domestic dispute intervention . . .

When are arrests made?

When called to domestic violence incidents, police officers' decision-making as to appropriate action is guided by their individual assessments of the situation which confronts them. The Association of Chief Police Officers of England, Wales and Northern Ireland, in their evidence to the Select Committee, said that decision-making should have regard to the following criteria:

1. the seriousness of the assault;
2. the availability of witnesses;
3. the character of the alleged assailant;
4. the age, infirmity etc of the complainant;
5. previous domestic history;
6. the wishes of the complainant;
7. whether, if prosecution ensued against the wishes of the complainant, the domestic situation would be adversely affected.

These factors, of course, constitute no more than guidelines and are subject to police officers' individual interpretation. Parnas (1967) has identified a number of factors important to that individual interpretation and decision-making:

1. the victim's motivation for calling the police (for example, is what is desired an arrest or a warning or the removal of the offender from the house?)
2. the impact of the offender's arrest on the victim;
3. the subcultural norms of the disputants;
4. the potential danger of more serious harm occurring on the offender's return;
5. the danger that arrest would jeopardise or terminate family relationships;
6. the possibility that the victim may change her mind regarding prosecution; and
7. the reluctance of prosecutors to handle domestic violence cases.

It should be noted that, prior to the establishment of the Crown Prosecution Service, the seventh factor was not relevant in the English context since police had responsibility for prosecutions. It is too early to know what impact the Crown Prosecution Service will have on the treatment of domestic violence cases and, in particular, on police practice. Pizzey (1974), Martin (1978) and Walker (1979) also suggest that officers are influenced by whether or not they have had similar experiences of domestic violence in their own families.

Humphreys and Humphreys (1985) take the view that police officers also make judgements as to the reason for the attack. In short, they decide — according to their own lights — whether the attack was warranted, whether there had been provocation, whether the victim had 'deserved' the treatment meted out and whether there were pressures which accounted for it. They draw the analogy of a bank robber who explains that he was forced into the robbery through losing his job, falling behind on credit payments, and needing to house, clothe and feed his family. If officers applied the same decision-making processes in this example as they do in domestic violence, some credence would have to be given to the robber's reasons (or rationalisations) for his behaviour. Continuing the analogy, the robber should be warned that if there was another occurrence then he would be arrested. Of course, this is unlikely to occur. Thus police decision-making in domestic violence incidents is seen as being intrinsically different from that involved in other types of crime.

Thus, not only are officers influenced by the formal policies of their forces, the training they have received, and the socialisation they experience into the ethos of their force, but they also carry with them to domestic scenes to which they are called their own views as to the 'appropriate' form of domestic relationships and, indeed, of women and what roles women should hold in society. These views influence whether they see the victim of domestic violence as being deserving of their help. The importance of the 'deserving victim' has been recorded in a number of research studies (see, for example, Davies, 1982; Dobash and Dobash, 1979; Fine, 1981). Ideas about wives' duties influence the judgement as to whether a female victim of domestic violence is a worthy recipient of help. For example, if there is evidence of poor housekeeping, of children not being as well looked after as they might be, or of meals not having been prepared when expected, these factors can have negative effects on the police officers' judgement of the victim for he may regard them as evidence of failing in 'wifely' duties. If the victim has been drinking, she is also likely to receive little sympathy.

The severity of injuries inflicted also affects the decision to arrest but is not the sole decisive factor (Dobash and Dobash, 1979; Edwards, 1986b). The research is replete with examples of quite serious injury which have nevertheless not led to police action in the form of arrest. It seems that both the British and American police operate an unofficial 'stitch' policy whereby if medical attention is required, especially for woundings, then police action will be taken, partly because of the severity of the violence but, Dobash and Dobash suggest, also partly because another agency, usually a hospital, has become involved.

It appears from Pahl's research (1982) that the police are more likely to adopt direct intervention tactics where a couple are either co-habiting but not married, or not actually still living together and are less likely to interfere in cases of married

46

couples still living together. The question of who calls the police for help is also of importance. Berk and Loseke (1980) and Dobash and Dobash (1979) both found that arrest was more likely when neighbours were sufficiently concerned or annoyed by the disturbance to call the police and to demand that something be done. The demeanour of a suspect has long been recognised as an important factor in the police decision whether or not to take action (Piliavin and Briar, 1969). This also applies in domestic violence incidents. If the assailant continues to be a nuisance after the police arrive, or challenges their authority in any way, or assaults a police officer then arrest is likely to ensue (Dobash and Dobash, 1979; Oppenlander, 1982). There is some evidence from the Dobashes' research and also from the London Strategic Policy Unit (1986) that sympathy from the police decreases the more often they are called to the same household and arrest becomes more unlikely. North American research, however, points in the opposite direction (see, for example, Burris and Jaffe, 1983).

Crisis intervention

If the police do not enforce the criminal law, it might be asked what do they do instead? Some, for example, Oppenlander (1982) have argued that the single most common police response is non-intervention, that is, officers state that there is nothing they can do and leave the incident to which they have been called. As has been shown above, a common response in this country is for the victim to be advised that it is not a matter for the criminal but for the civil law. Alternatively, and/or additionally, victims might be advised to take a private prosecution for common assault.

Other responses have also been observed. The most common are attempts to cool or to defuse the situation; to threaten with future arrest if there is a re-occurrence of the incident; and to remove one of the parties, often the female victim, from the scene for a time (Parnas, 1971). Defusing the situation by 'talking to' the parties, trying to reason with and get them to agree as to the error of their ways is done often in an informal way by individual officers taking this role upon themselves without necessarily having the benefit of training as to how it can best be achieved. This certainly seems to have been the case in Britain until at least the early 1980s. Prior to then, training courses dwelt primarily upon the legal aspects of domestic violence: criteria for different types of assault; injunctions with or without a power of arrest; breach of the peace; and rights of entry. Since then, however, considerably more attention has been paid to the need for training in social skills and in the management of conflict. Dealing with domestic violence is included within these courses. Without the benefit of such training, officers had to resort to what might be regarded as 'common sense' and not necessarily practical advice — 'learn to live together', 'avoid confrontation'. It appears that despite the new training, this type of advice-giving can still prevail (Horton and Smith, 1988).

The management of domestic violence by techniques of crisis intervention gained popularity particularly in the United States and Canada where special training programmes were developed (see Parnas, 1967; Bard and Zacker, 1971; Bard, 1973). The development of programmes was rapid. In 1966, no police department offered special training: three years later almost every large police department and many of the smaller ones did (Leibman and Schwartz, 1972). The basic idea behind the training courses was to broaden the range of responses of individual officers to domestic violence and to help them to distinguish incidents where a law enforcement function was clearly required from those where it might be possible to achieve a peaceful solution. An important purpose of the latter was to try to ensure that the likelihood of future violence was reduced through the involvement of other community agencies and techniques such as mediation.

A number of different models of crisis intervention techniques have been developed. Some, as in Bard's well known New York initiative, have relied upon the training of specialist officers (Bard, 1970); some have relied on police-social work teams as in London, Ontario (Jaffe and Thompson, 1982); some have used teams of police and trained volunteers as in Restigouche, Canada (Lerette, 1984) and yet others have simply relied upon general training for all officers (as appears to be the case in Britain). The question arises as to whether such techniques work, although this begs the question of what criteria are to be used to assess effectiveness. Studies which have examined crisis intervention programmes have tended to use different measures — lower arrest rates, increased police safety, officers' perceptions of and satisfaction with the programmes and so on. It is thus difficult to form firm conclusions though there are many critics who suggest that such schemes are deliberately used as a means of arrest avoidance (for example, Loving and Farmer, 1980). Oppenlander (1982) goes further: she says such schemes are "victim aversive". Even Parnas, originally an enthusiastic advocate, has doubted the ideological basis of programmes which assume that therapy is the most appropriate response. In 1977 in a paper to the International Society of Family Law (quoted in Freeman, 1979) he took the view that:

> There is simply no evidence that we know how to diagnose much less treat disputants' problems in a manner that will prevent repetition.

Bard's specialist police training programme, perhaps because it was the first to train police officers in crisis intervention and attracted considerable publicity, has been subject to considerable scrutiny. Although it failed to show a reduction in violence overall, it was nevertheless claimed as a success, partly because it was said to have reduced violence towards police officers while handling domestic incidents and partly because arrest rates fell. The claim of decreased violence to police officers has, however, been disputed by Leibman and Schwartz (1972). Further criticisms have been made, most notably by Loving and Farmer (1980). These include:

1. failing to monitor long term follow-up effects on the families dealt with under the programme;
2. failing to distinguish which skills were particularly apt for which types of violent incidents;

3. failing to determine which individual skills could identify the type of officer best suited for such specialist deployment;
4. failing to distinguish assaults where arrest would be the most appropriate strategy, and
5. failing to monitor subsequent handling of cases either in the courts or through other means such as social work and counselling.

Loving and Quirk (1982) have gone further in their criticisms of crisis intervention techniques, particularly in cases where serious injury or repeated abuse has occurred. They take the view that such strategies may aggravate the problem by suggesting to assailants that their violent behaviour can be overlooked.

In Canada, a somewhat different system has been employed. The most well-known is that developed in London, Ontario, which includes crisis intervention training for all police officers plus a family consultant service which acts as specialists with the police on family dispute calls.[2] The initiative was started in 1972 by the London Police Department which was concerned by the workload caused by 'domestic trouble' calls and felt that traditional police methods were failing to tackle the problem effectively. At first, the counsellors who were hired by the police were not part of the police department but acted as consultants who were on call at the request of police officers to provide immediate crisis counselling and undertake referral functions. That initial 'independence' helped gain support from other professional agencies in the community and allowed the consultants to act as brokers between the police and other services. In 1976, the experiment having been judged a success, the family consultant service was established as a permanent civilian branch of the police force. The counsellors operate from 9 a.m. to 4 a.m. but provide cover especially during evenings and weekends when other specialist services are not available[3]. Officers leave the scene of the domestic violence when the consultant has been briefed — unless it is thought likely that violence will again shortly ensue — and the consultants take over mediation/counselling and referral funcions. Jaffe and Thompson (1982) claim that police experience in handling crisis situations has steadily improved and that the number of repeat calls to the police, especially in chronic cases, has decreased. Whether the latter should be taken as a sign of success is, of course, debatable for there may be other reasons for failing to make calls, but, overall, the initiative is deemed a success (Ontario Status of Women Council, 1980). Jaffe, Thompson and Wolfe (1984) compared families who had experienced family consultant intervention with those who had received police intervention only. They concluded that the former group were better

---

[2] There have been numerous publications on the work of the London, Ontario, family consultant service. Readers may wish to consult, *inter alia,* Babin (1985); Burris and Jaffe (1983, 1984); Jaffe and Thompson (1978, 1982, and 1984); Jaffe, Thompson and Pacquin (1978); Jaffe, Thompson and Wolfe (1984); Jaffe *et al.* (1986a and b); and Reitz 1974).

[3] The role of the consultant service has expanded over the years to embrace problems other than domestic violence — for example problems relating to the care and management of children who come to the attention of the police; and problems experienced by depressed or suicidal individuals and by the elderly.

adjusted and functioning at a higher level in terms of reasoning ability and lack of verbal aggression in dealing with family problems.

From its inception, there was clear recognition that solutions cannot be provided by one programme or indeed one part of a system: a multi-dimensional solution had to be devised. Since 1979 the initiative in London, Ontario, has been guided by a co-ordinating committee comprising representatives from the criminal justice and social service systems as well as other local groups (Jaffe and Burris, 1984). The committee provided a forum both for the exchange of information, including research findings, and for the operationalisation of recommendations for community action. It served, too, to co-ordinate the services available. From the outset it was assumed that the criminal justice system *should* be the primary system for dealing with domestic violence. Moreover, it was further assumed that the response of the criminal justice system required most improvement. However, given the nature of the problem, the involvement of a variety of other agencies — medical, educational, social work — was seen as likely to enhance effectiveness and therefore there was a perceived need for the integration and co-ordination of responses. This was borne out by the committee's experience of working together. The process facing a victim wanting protection was discovered to be very much a game of chance. Even within the criminal justice system itself, various agents had conflicting policies, both formal and informal, and victims were the recipients of much conflicting advice.

Under the aegis of the committee, a number of important experiments were set up. These included:

1. establishing a treatment programme for assailants;
2. providing victims with an information card giving not only the officer's name (so that he might be contacted for further advice) but also addresses and telephone numbers of appropriate agencies and an outline of possible sources of action;
3. educational campaigns to sensitize professionals in the community — physicians, psychiatrists, therapists, social workers and clergy — to the problems faced by domestic violence victims and their need for help;
4. a publicity campaign to inform members of the public of changes in policy and of the reasons for and objectives of these changes; and
5. establishing a victim advocacy service to provide legal assistance, advocacy and emotional support counselling.

Fundamental to the work of the Co-ordinating Committee is the continued identification of gaps in service provision, the development of new programmes and the avoidance of duplication of services and/or of competition between agencies for scarce resources. Within the last two years, children's programmes and advocacy services have been initiated for children living at the Women's Community House (refuge). In addition, group counselling for children exposed to domestic violence is offered through the Family Court Clinic. Throughout its history, the Committee has encouraged research evaluations of its initiatives.

One of the most important innovations involved the police. In 1981 police officers were instructed to lay common assault charges in all cases of domestic violence where they had reasonable and probable grounds to believe that an offence had occurred. This initiative, therefore, removed the onus of laying charges from the victim. In the first four months of the new policy in 1981, 38 common assault charges were laid by the police whereas in the first six months of 1979 no such charge had been laid. Moreover, the policy change not only affected the laying of common assault charges but brought about a change in charges of assault occasioning bodily harm: 32 charges were laid by the police in this period compared with only six charges in the first six months of 1979. A later evaluation by Jaffe *et al.* (1986c) has shown that the policy change resulted in a 2,500% increase in police-laid charges from the 1979 base-line (pre-policy) to the end of 1983. Burris and Jaffe (1983) have argued that this is evidence that traditional police attitudes to domestic violence which result in their non-enforcement of the criminal law can be changed provided that they have clear policy guidelines encouraging decisive action. In Jaffe *et al.*'s later work (1986c), however, the conclusion is more cautious: changes in police behaviour are seen as dramatic, changes in attitude more ambivalent.

The research conducted by Burris and Jaffe (1983) and by Jaffe *et al.* (1986c) also examined a number of other important aspects stemming from the policy change. Contrary to the belief that victims would be less co-operative, they found that police laying charges resulted in a significant decrease in women seeking to withdraw charges and an increase in victim satisfaction with police action. Moreover, a significant reduction (as measured by victims' self report data) was found in all forms of violence occurring in the twelve month period following the police laying charges compared to the preceding twelve month period. Nevertheless, Jaffe *et al.* (1986c) note that although a 'strong' police response appears to be a strong deterrent in the majority of cases, violence was not entirely eliminated. This reinforces the belief that the problem of domestic violence cannot be successfully tackled by reliance on any one particular intervention. Moreover, victims of domestic violence expressed considerable dissatisfaction with the level of support given by Crown Attorneys whilst the majority of police officers felt that the courts did not support police policies. Whether those last two findings would still hold good if the research were replicated now is impossible to judge. The Jaffe *et al.* (1986c) study was carried out in 1983 since when a number of additional changes have been made. The Battered Women's Advocacy Clinic which offers support to victims of domestic violence throughout court proceedings and which liaises with the Crown Attorney Office was not started until 1983, the year of the Jaffe *et al.* (1986c) study. Moreover, the London Crown Attorney has since supported efforts to make the court process more supportive to victims (for example through the use of Victim Impact Statements) in addition to taking a strong stand against allowing the dropping of charges. Since 1984 the Ministries of the Solicitor General and Attorney General for Ontario have also instituted special training programmes on domestic violence for Crown Attorneys; encouraged the appointment of special

Domestic Assault Prosecutors; issued guidelines on the handling of such cases and, in particular, on the question of victims' wishing to withdraw charges; and set up a research programme to evaluate the use of Victim Impact Statements.[4]

The London, Ontario, model of crisis intervention does not, therefore, rest solely on mediation by police officers or other specialists, nor does it start from the assumption that the criminal law and its enforcement is inappropriate to domestic violence. On the contrary, its basic premise was that the criminal justice system was *the* most appropriate system but that solutions would have to go wider than mere invocation of criminal law processes; victims' needs extended beyond that and the machinery of the criminal law would be ineffective if not backed by a host of other measures. In short, an integrated response by the whole community was required.

It appears that in Britain, too, crisis intervention is seen as the most appropriate response of the police. Edwards' (1986b and d) interviews with police officers revealed that they saw their role as to 'cool', 'calm', or 'defuse' the situation. These interviews also revealed that officers felt uncomfortable in their role: many were young and felt they lacked credibility in such matters. Others thought that they should not be doing 'social work'. There was thus a marked tendency, in addition to advising that civil remedies were the appropriate solution, to allow a 'cooling off' period after the victim had said she wanted a charge to be made.

Putting aside the example of London, Ontario, there is a general view that crisis intervention which relies upon negotiation, mediation, 'talking to', does not work. Buchanan and Chasnoff (1986) carried out a review of family crisis intervention programmes and concluded that, although there was anecdotal evidence of increased officer training skills, such evidence did not rise above the level of the anecdote: most studies showed no real effect. Moreover, only in Washington DC was there a decrease in assaults on police officers. Bae (1981) takes the view that crisis intervention techniques indicate a lack of concern with victims' safety and reflect that the problem is not regarded as serious and, therefore, does not warrant serious investigation. There is as yet no convincing evidence that crisis intervention, based on mediation techniques, can produce any long-term reductions in domestic violence (Pearce and Snortum, 1983). Edwards (1986d) in Britain also thinks that such techniques are 'largely ineffective'. Sometimes this is thought to be due to inept application of such skills. The police are thought to appear unsympathetic (Roy, 1977) and even at times to side with the assailant (Parnas, 1967; Straus *et al.* 1980). It should be noted, however, that a recent study in this country (Horton and Smith, 1988) which involved observation of police handling of 'domestic disputes' (including family, neighbour and landlord/tenant disputes) found no evidence of taking sides unless one of the parties was clearly committing an offence. Nor were officers seen to pass judgements on the incident in front of the two parties involved.

---

[4] Correspondence with Ministries of Attorney General and Solicitor General, Ontario.

Referrals to other agencies

A central part of crisis intervention should involve referral to other agencies, but this appears to occur only rarely. Edwards (1986b and d), for example, concluded that police officers lacked not only basic information on local agencies, but also did not have the resources to ensure adequate referrals. Moreover, liaison between the police and other agencies — social services, Citizens Advice Bureaux, National Association of Victim Support Schemes, Women's Aid and so forth — in the two areas she studied was found to be poor. Where advice was given to consult another agency, there was a tendency to overplay the role of the Citizens Advice Bureaux and, by comparison, Women's Aid was seldom suggested. Indeed, some of the officers interviewed by Edwards had no knowledge at all of the refuge movement yet Women's Aid caters exclusively for domestic violence victims. Others regarded the organisation as "diametrically opposed to police interests" (Edwards, 1986c).

American research also confirms the low rate of referral to other social services (Loving and Farmer, 1980). In Brown's (1984) study of 84 domestic violence victims seeking admission to a refuge for battered wives only a few (6%) had received advice on referrals to other agencies. Yet in Bell's (1984) study almost all of the officers who completed a questionnaire (N=41) agreed with the statement: "The police officer should make sure the woman knows about shelter homes and should see she is able to get to one". Moreover, more than four fifths agreed that "Referring the man and/or woman to counselling is often a good thing for the police officer to do". However, referrals to other agencies were actually made in only about a fifth of cases. Oppenlander (1982) had previously found that such referrals were in fact less common than arrests. Although 90% of the officers she interviewed claimed knowledge of referral agencies and almost half said they routinely made such referrals whilst about another third claimed to do so sometimes, Oppenlander's observation of police action revealed that referrals to social service agencies occurred in very few (4%) cases.

Underlying Attitudes

Danger to the police

One of the explanations advanced, at least in the United States, for police inaction and reluctance to become involved in domestic violence is that such incidents are believed to present a real danger to officers' personal safety. Thus Parnas (1971)[5] has said:

> The physical risk involved in domestic disputes is extreme . . . more officers have been killed or injured responding to these kinds of incidents during the last ten years than in responding to any other traditional police call for service.

---

5 Parnas (1971) also noted that police training programmes placed more stress on the perceived dangers than on the dynamics of domestic violence *per se*.

FBI statistics (1978) seemed to show some support for this view. It was estimated there that just under a third of all assaults committed against police officers arose during the course of 'domestic disputes'. Moreover, a fifth of officers' deaths between 1973 and 1977 were thought to have occurred in response to 'domestic disturbance' calls. This view of the danger to police officers has been reiterated more recently by Straus, Gelles and Steinmetz (1980). A recent survey by Dolon et al. (1986) of police officers' attitudes also revealed that domestic violence was regarded as a threat to safety.

Garner and Clemmer (1986) have, however, re-analysed the United States evidence and concluded that the danger to police has been overstated — a conclusion also reached by Ellis (1987). Previously, data on all 'disturbance' calls have been interpreted as solely or primarily comprising 'domestic disturbances'. Garner and Clemmer (1986) found, however, that in fact domestic incidents comprised only a small part of general disturbance calls (which included bar fights, fights between gangs, general disturbances short of civil disorder or riot, and citizens brandishing firearms) and, when domestic incidents were separated out, the data revealed that fewer deaths were actually associated with domestic assignments than with other types of disturbance calls. (Robbery calls were found to be the most consistently dangerous.) Garner and Clemmer concluded that the proportion of deaths occurring in domestic incidents was less than one third the number commonly suggested in earlier literature. Moreover, not only were the number of deaths less than previously reported but, given the frequency with which such domestic assignments occur, domestic incidents were proportionately less likely to result in officers' deaths. Garner and Clemmer suggested, therefore, that the notion that 'domestic disturbance' calls resulted in a large number of police deaths ought to be abandoned. Ellis (1987) has pointed out that it is not just the risk of death which has been exaggerated but also the risk of assault or injury. He found (using US data) that for every police officer assaulted during 1982-83 while attending a domestic disturbance, five were assaulted while responding to a non-family disturbance and that domestic disturbances accounted for only about 6% of all deaths and injuries to police officers. He, too, therefore concludes that the notion of 'dangerousness' should be discarded.

'Not police work'

The lack of effective action by the police has also been attributed to the view that police officers do not believe that dealing with domestic violence is 'proper' police work. This is closely allied to the view that domestic violence is not 'properly criminal' but is rather a matter for the civil law — if for the law at all. Pahl (1982a) and Borkowski et al. (1983), for example, report that much domestic violence is regarded by the police as trivial. Edwards (1986d) has said that it is only if it goes 'right over the top' that it is regarded as a matter requiring, and deserving of police attention. The police view is encapsulated in the evidence of a senior police officer to the Select Committee who offered the opinion that arrest would not "answer the problem''. But, as Sanders (1987) has noted, this criterion of usefulness is rarely applied — perhaps except in white collar crime — in most areas of crime where ''arrest, charge and prosecution is routine''. More recently — in an often quoted comment — an Assistant Commissioner of the Metropolitan Police suggested categorising ''domestic disputes'' with ''stranded people, lost property and stray animals'' as tasks to be handed over to other agencies to relieve the police for ''crime prevention, detection and community policing — real crime work'' (The Times, 4 October 1983). Southgate (1986) also reports that the police define requests for help with ''lost dogs, domestic disputes, rowdy youth and bothersome drunks'', as ''rubbish work''. As has been noted, Edwards (1986d) found resentment amongst police officers that they should have to do ''social work''. Faragher (1985) similarly records the police view that such work ''should not really have concerned us''. There are signs, however, that domestic violence is now to be given a higher priority among some police forces. Following a report by an internal working group, the Metropolitan Police have issued new guidelines to officers which call for domestic violence assaults to be treated as seriously as assaults occurring in the street (Jesperson, 1987).

The view that domestic violence is not 'police work' is not peculiar to Britain. Similar themes have also been found in research from the United States. Both Loving and Farmer (1980) and Parnas (1971), for example, have commented that 'domestic dispute' calls are not seen as real police work but as a nuisance. Bell (1985) states that the police argue that they are not marriage counsellors or social workers. Yet a great deal of police work is taken up with activities which do not centre upon the 'good pinch' or 'collars'. A number of both British and North American studies have pointed out that arrest is a rare occurrence during the ordinary course of officers' duties (for example, Banton, 1964; Black, 1971; and Bittner, 1974), whilst Morgan (1980) and Punch and Naylor (1973) have shown that almost a half of police time is concerned with peacekeeping and social welfare roles.

'Not criminal'

The view that the police should not be involved in dealing with domestic violence reveals an underlying assumption that such violence is not 'truly' criminal in the same way that violence between those who are not related is regarded as 'truly criminal'. Advice to victims to use the available civil law remedies reflects the belief that domestic violence is an inappropriate area in which to invoke the criminal law. The rationale for this seems to lie in the notion that domestic violence is almost exclusively a 'family matter' or a 'private affair' in which state intervention has no business since it would constitute not solely an intrusion into a private relationship but also an erosion of individual liberties (see, *inter alia*, Dobash and Dobash, 1979; Faragher, 1985; McCabe and Sutcliffe, 1978; Pahl, 1982a, 1985). The integrity of the family unit is seen as paramount. It might be questioned whether this respect for the privacy and integrity of the family unit should extend to permitting physical violence within the confines of the family for, as Sanders (1987) has commented, keeping the family intact is achieved at the expense of the victim's physical integrity. Or, as Faragher (1985) has expressed the same sentiment: "Whose privacy? Whose liberty?". Freeman (1985b) takes the view that it is the public/private dichotomy which is "at the root of a critical theory of family law". He, too, believes that the public/private distinctions serves to deny protection to women and that non-intervention strategies which are shaped by such distinctions serve to protect the dominance of men against women: "Privacy is not. . . an absolute: the privacy of some is more inviolate than others". Like Faragher (1985) Freeman poses the questions: "Whose privacy is it? How is it defined? Who uses it?"

Edwards (1986d) goes further in her explanation of police responses to domestic violence. On the basis of her interviews with police officers, she concludes that domestic violence is regarded as a normal occurrence within family life. The more serious incidents merely reflect overstepping the boundaries of arguably acceptable and thus permitted levels of physical violence. It was only when this happened, for example, where a weapon was used and serious injury inflicted, that there was seen to be a legitimate need for police involvement.

Not all officers see domestic violence as a problem about which there ought to be no concern. Indeed, a number of researchers have recorded the genuine concern and sympathy felt for victims (McCabe and Sutcliffe, 1978; Dobash and Dobash, 1979). Rather it is a problem about which distinctions seem to be drawn between its social and its criminal nature. There seems to be an assumption that preserving family relationships is indeed the most — if not the only — desirable outcome. Furthermore, this outcome is seen as likely to be achieved by social service agencies or through civil law remedies and not by the police. Dobash and Dobash (1979) have criticised this as merely providing a rationale for inaction. Such a solution is also dependent upon social service agencies accepting such a definition. They may, however, have their own definition of the problem as a police matter. If so — and the response of social service agencies will be examined later — victims could find themselves passed from agency to agency with none accepting responsibility in the sense of providing practical, concrete advice and assistance.

'Victim reluctance'

A common reason discerned in both British and in North American research literature to explain the lack of police intervention is that of 'victim reluctance' or 'reliability' — that is the belief that the victim will withdraw the complaint and the couple will continue to live in their relationship or get back together again. The police believe that women call for their assistance not so much from a wish to pursue legal action, but from a desire for immediate protection and, perhaps also, from the hope that a police presence will act as a warning or deterrent to their husbands or cohabitants (Johnson, 1985). Although it has been shown that women do in fact often ask the police to arrest their assailants (see, for example, Bowker, 1982 and Pagelow, 1981a), nevertheless there continues to be a strong belief in the police that this will be a fruitless exercise since, as Faragher (1985) puts it:

It is part of the common wisdom of the police station, reinforced through the training school, that women will inevitably withdraw their complaints and will fail to co-operate in legal proceedings.

Edwards (1986d) argues that this belief influences police action from the outset. 'Criming' domestic violence was, for example, regarded as a "waste of time".

Stanko (1985) has claimed that 'victim reluctance' is a myth. That is perhaps too overstated a view. It is unquestionably true that some women do withdraw their complaints, but the evidence is unclear as to how frequently they do so. In Edwards' (1986d) study of those incidents for which the police initially made out a crime report, almost all (96%) of the four fifths of cases which were later 'no crimed' were on the grounds that the complainant withdrew the allegation. In the Bedfordshire police initiative in 1976, it was found that, after talking to the parties at the time of the initial intervention by the police, almost two thirds of victims decided not to pursue their complaints. In a study by Bowden (quoted in Cannings, 1984) carried out in the Greater Manchester police in 1978, half of the victims later withdrew their initial complaints. Other studies have, however, suggested much lower withdrawal rates: Faragher (1985) reports a 1 in 10 withdrawal; Dobash and Dobash (1979) found that only 6% of the women in their study dropped their allegations prior to final adjudication; Wasoff (1982) reported that, out of 59 cases, only one request to withdraw was made by a women who was the victim of domestic violence (the request was refused). Sanders (1987) (who found a domestic violence withdrawal rate of 10%) has usefully drawn attention to the fact that withdrawals of complaints are also made by victims in non-domestic violence cases: although domestic violence victims were more likely to withdraw prior to the decision to prosecute, after that decision had been made they were less likely to do so than non-domestic violence victims. Sanders also found that even where the police had reservations about the 'reliability' or 'reluctance of victims' in non-domestic violence cases, they nevertheless went ahead with the prosecution. By contrast, withdrawal of complaints in all domestic violence cases was sufficient for them not to prosecute. Sanders concluded that this was further evidence of:

> The police appear[ing] to believe that victims of domestic violence are *fundamentally* unreliable and unpredictable...

Research has also shown that the police can, in fact, be instrumental in influencing whether a complaint is withdrawn (see, for example, Chambers and Miller, 1983). It has already been noted that the police often allow a 'cooling off' period, a chance to 'think matters over' in the belief that this will result in unemotional decisions being made. Faragher (1985) records that victims are asked repeatedly if they *really* wish to take legal action. This might well influence the victim's decision. They may interpret the question as a lack of police support which, if, as seems likely, there is already fear of retaliation, could well tip the balance in favour of withdrawal of the complaint. Furthermore, both the Wasoff (1982) and Dobash and Dobash (1979) research referred to earlier indicated that, at least in their studies, withdrawals were requested and/or made only after lengthy court delays which served to augment women's sense of isolation and perceived lack of support — in short, a perceived indifference of the legal system.

Comparing male and female police officers' attitudes

Edwards' (1986b and d) interviews with police officers indicated that there was a general view that female officers and older married male officers were better suited to cases of domestic violence. There have been few studies specifically examining differences in attitudes between the sexes. A notable exception is the work in the United States of Homant and Kennedy (1985) who administered a self-completion questionnaire to 62 policewomen and 89 policemen. The impetus for their study came from their earlier work (1983) which had revealed that 31 of the female victims of domestic violence in their sample of 90 who had at least one experience of a policewoman responding to their call for assistance were more likely to express satisfaction with the police intervention than those who had never been attended by a female officer. Moreover, policewomen were regarded as more 'capable' and the victims hoped that at least one female officer would respond should they need help in the future. Homant and Kennedy, therefore, set out to investigate whether the women's perceived differences were only that — a matter of perception — or whether there was a difference between male and female officers in terms of attitudes and perceptions about the nature of domestic violence. Homant and Kennedy also examined the question of how policewomen were thought to respond to domestic violence incidents. They found that policewomen were more concerned about domestic violence. This was partly accounted for by higher educational levels among female officers but, when those were controlled for, gender differences still existed. There were also differences in how the two groups perceived the nature of policewomen's responses. Female officers saw themselves as being more patient and understanding, less likely to exacerbate the situation, whereas male officers criticised women officers for lacking what they saw as the necessary assertiveness.

Arrest as a preventive measure

The many criticisms made of the apparent non-arrest policies of the police have already been noted. It will suffice here, therefore, merely to reiterate the view that such policies may signify to assailants that their behaviour is not really regarded as criminal. Conversely, it can be argued that a vigorous arrest policy would demonstrate social disapproval and might act as a deterrent to further violence. Some evidence in support of this view has already been discussed (*supra* p51) in relation to the evaluation by Jaffe *et al.* (1986c) of the impact of police 'laying charges' in London, Ontario. They concluded that a strong law enforcement response did act as a deterrent to further violence when measured both by repeat calls to the police for assistance and by victims' self report data. Further Canadian research by Dutton (1987) predicts that although arrest can act as a deterrent, its effects are likely to be short-term unless coupled with other legal sanctions. Based on a small sample of twenty four men convicted of common assault against their wives, he found that, over time (one and a half years), there was a significant decrease in their perceived likelihood and severity of justice sanctions compared to their perception shortly after conviction. In an earlier study, however, Dutton (1986) concluded that the deterrent effect of arrest could be enhanced by the use of court mandated treatment programmes for male abusers. Over a two and a half year period following arrest, he demonstrated that a group of non-treated abusers had a re-arrest rate of 40% compared to 4% for treated abusers. Moreover, more then four fifths of the wives of men who had participated in treatment programmes reported no acts of severe violence towards them in the follow-up period.

Evidence from the United States also suggests that arrest may indeed act as a deterrent. Jolin (1983), for example, has attributed a discerned downward trend in domestic homicides in Oregon to a pro-arrest police policy effected in 1977 when — subject to the proviso that the victim did not object — officers were instructed that they must arrest where there was probable cause that an assault had occurred or where it appeared that serious physical injury was threatened. Pence (1983), reporting on the Domestic Abuse Intervention Project in Duluth, Minnesota, (which began in 1981 and which was therefore one of the earliest initiatives in the United States adopting an inter-agency approach but with an emphasis on a criminal justice response) also records an apparent deterrent effect of arrest when measured by repeat calls to the police (no victim self-report data were collected). Using this measure, however, she found — contrary to Dutton's (1986) conclusion — that the deterrent effect was sustained over a twelve month period and in fact that repeat calls fell from 38% in the first six months following arrest to 16% in the second six month period.

The most well known study and arguably, the most important so far available, however, is the work of Sherman and Berk (1984) in Minneapolis. Its importance lies in its attempt to evaluate a random experiment to test which of three police responses — arrest, separation of the parties, and advice which could, at the officers' discretion, include mediation and counselling — was most effective in deterring subsequent violence over a six month follow-up period. The experiment was conducted in the two Minneapolis precincts which had the highest levels of domestic violence crime reports and arrests. It did not include the more serious types of domestic violence involving life-threatening or severe injury (felonies) but was limited in its application to simple (misdeameanour) assaults. Only volunteer officers took part in the experiment. Under the design of the study, each officer's response to a simple domestic assault was predetermined by means of a colour-coded pad of report forms indicating the three different types of permissible responses: action in any individual case was determined by the colour of the top form on the pad. The experiment ran for a period of approximately eighteen months and produced some 300 cases for analysis. Effectiveness was measured by means of police records of subsequent violence reported to them and a series of twelve follow-up interviews (both face-to-face and telephone interviews) with victims. Both measures showed arrest to be the most effective strategy in preventing repeat incidents over the six month follow-up period. Official police records showed separation as the least effective, whilst advice was revealed as the least effective in the victims' interviews. It is also worthy of note that of the 136 arrested offenders, only 3 were formally punished by the courts. Sherman and Berk conclude from this that arrest and initial incarceration — irrespective of subsequent prosecution and sentencing — can act as deterrents in themselves.

This research evidence appears to have been highly influential in shaping stated police policies in the United States. A telephone survey of 173 urban police departments serving cities of populations of over 100,000 was carried out by Sherman *et al.* (1986) in 1984 and repeated one year later. They found that in 1984 only one in ten of the departments had instituted policies encouraging arrest in cases of domestic violence; the proportion had risen to almost a third at the time of the 1985 survey. Moreover, the later survey revealed that two thirds of the departments contacted were familiar with the results of the Minneapolis study. The survey was again repeated in 1986 and by that point almost a half of the police departments reported that arrest was their preferred policy (Cohn and Sherman, 1987). How far these stated policies have brought about changes in police practice is, however, more doubtful. Kaufman Kantor and Straus (1987a), using interview data from the 1985 US nationally representative sample of over 6,000 American families, found that arrest was a far from typical police response — occurring in only a fifth of *severe* wife assaults. They state that although "he practice of favouring arrests may be spreading. . .little has actually changed". The 1985 survey was also analysed to shed light on the abusers' perspective of legal and other sanctions. This revealed that both arrest and the possibility of their wives leaving were seen as highly unlikely which led Kaufman Kantor and Straus (1987a) to conclude that:

> part of the reason men beat their wives is because they can get away with it. . .Until the probability of assault increases, abusers will continue to receive a *de facto* message that they can assault their wives and get away with it.

Sherman and Berk (1984) reject the idea of mandatory arrest, favouring instead a presumption in favour of arrest unless there are 'good clear reasons' why it would be non-productive. Others, however, (for example, Humphreys and Humphreys, 1985) have called for mandatory arrest policies despite the fact that Sherman and Berk's findings should be regarded as tentative until the experiment has been replicated fully elsewhere. Replications are indeed underway, funded by the National Institute of Justice. Until those evaluations have been completed there remains only indirect support — in addition to the Canadian and Duluth research — for the Minneapolis findings. Berk and Newton (1985) did not utilise a randomised experiment technique, but relied upon an analysis of almost 800 cases of domestic violence coming to the notice of the police in a southern Californian county over a 28 month period. Arrests were made in just over a quarter of the incidents and Berk and Newton argue that they did act as a deterrent to the commission of further offences.

Given the attention Sherman and Berk's (1984) study has attracted, it is perhaps especially important to consider its limitations, some of which are recognised by the researchers themselves (Berk and Sherman, 1985). First, there were a number of ways in which the design of the random experiment was undermined. Officers were given the right to vary a separation or advice response in certain circumstances: where, for example, the offender would not leave the premises when ordered to; if the officers were assaulted; if a restraining order was violated; or if the victim persistently demanded that the offender be arrested. Leaving that aside, Sherman and Berk (1984) admit that many of the officers failed to follow fully the randomised experimental design. All attempts made to monitor its implementation failed. Although self-report data can usefully augment information from official police records, the actual response rates achieved in this part of the study were disappointing. At the time of the initial interview, almost two thirds of victims responded but there was a continuing gradual drop until just under half took part in the last interview. Moreover, Berk and Sherman (1985) report that interviewers formed the impression that victims were under-reporting new incidents of violence.

Other, more general, points can also be made. The findings may not, for example, be generalisable to other cities: Sherman and Berk (1984) say that "Minneapolis is hardly representative of all urban areas". Since the study relied upon volunteer officers, who presumably would be unlikely to want to undermine the study (and yet who nevertheless failed to follow the randomised design in all cases), it is impossible to generalise from their actions to other police officers. Furthermore, had it been possible to monitor the officers' implementation of the random design through observation, this would have made it possible to also collect information on *how* the officers dealt with the incident and whether their manner of doing so affected outcomes. Ethical reasons prevented the experiment from encompassing within its ambit the more serious incidents of domestic violence. This poses the question whether the results would hold for those incidents. It may also be the case that arrest is a more effective deterrent for different types of offender — for example, men who do not have a long history of abusing their partners or perhaps men who have not previously experienced any officer reaction other than a 'talking to'. Such information would help inform police strategies as to the selective use of arrest. The suggestion that arrest should be used routinely on its own as a deterrent without subsequent recourse to prosecution in the courts might well be a matter for concern as such practices may undermine civil liberties. Although arrest has been claimed as a deterrent, more needs to be known about the precise mechanisms by which it deters. If, for example, it is through the reinforcement of anti-battering norms then it is arguable that increased prosecution and more severe sentences could act as further reinforcement. Or, if, as Gelles (1983) has argued, domestic violence ensues from the 'rewards' of actions not being outweighed by 'costs', then prosecution and punishment might also be seen as adding to the cost incurred in being arrested.

The Metropolitan Police Force initiative

As a result of a Working Party review of their handling of domestic violence, the Metropolitan Police Force issued a force order in June 1987 which encouraged the use of arrest in domestic violence incidents. The order also recommended that officers involve other agencies in seeking solutions and initiatives to domestic violence cases; that they be prepared to offer constructive and compassionate advice; and that police transport should be used wherever possible to take women and children to refuges. As a result of this order, one police station, Tottenham, has set up a special programme to initiate a multi-agency approach to tackling the problem of domestic violence (Horley, 1988). As yet there is no research evidence available on how the new force order or the Tottenham initiative are working.

8 The prosecution process

By comparison with the degree of attention which has been devoted to the police, research on prosecution, the courts and sentencing practice in relation to domestic violence remains a relatively neglected area. What evidence exists suggests that the decision to prosecute is a fairly rare occurrence. In Edwards' (1986b) study, for example, only 17 cases out of her sample of 773 domestic violence incidents reported to the police were finally proceeded with. This low rate of prosecution has also been discerned in North America. Despite considerable 'screening out' of less serious assaults by police officers, prosecutors nevertheless have refused to prosecute in the majority of cases actually reaching their attention (US Commission on Civil Rights, 1983). MacLeod's (1983) large scale study also revealed that prosecutors often recommended that a case be *nolle prossed*, prosecuted as a misdemeanour rather than as a felony, or handled through the civil courts or by social services. Grim (1983) has noted that although Ohio's Domestic Violence Act is among the most comprehensive of recent legislation in the United States to combat family violence, nevertheless, in many parts of the state, 'the intended benefits have been largely unrealised'. Martin (1976) has commented that the 'counting stitches' practice operated by the police also operates in district attorneys' prosecution decisions. Furthermore, the 'stitches rule' is coupled with a requirement that there should be witnesses to an assault. Since there are rarely witnesses to domestic violence, prosecutions are infrequent and are usually restricted to those cases judged by the district attorney to have a good chance of conviction (Humphreys and Humphreys, 1985).

The discussion *supra* (pp53-58) of the underlying attitudes which help influence police actions in relation to domestic violence is also pertinent to a discussion of prosecution decisions. Until the advent of the Crown Prosecution Service, such decisions were made in England and Wales by the police themselves: other countries, such as Scotland, have a rather long history of a public prosecution system. The factors influencing police decisions to 'crime' domestic violence incidents and to arrest offenders are, by extension, also relevant to the decision to prosecute. Those factors include the belief that domestic violence victims are intrinsically unreliable, will withdraw complaints and fail to co-operate in any prosecution; the belief that much domestic violence is of a trivial nature; the view that domestic violence victims are usually 'undeserving'; and the belief that it is a family matter in which the law should not interfere.

Sanders (1987) has advanced a rather different explanation as to why domestic violence is treated differently from violence between strangers. From his large study of prosecution decision-making, he obtained a very small sample of domestic and non-domestic violence cases which allowed him to compare police officers' and prosecutors' decision-making in respect of each group. He discovered that many of the non-domestic violence cases concerned public order and it is this factor which he suggests is the important predictor of whether a prosecution will go ahead. This does not mean, however, that he did not find differences between the two groups which would lend some support to the explanations proffered by other researchers. For example, where concern existed over the reliability of the victim in non-domestic violence cases, this — unlike cases of domestic violence — did not influence the decision to go ahead with the prosecution. Withdrawal of a complaint in a domestic violence case always led to non-prosecution, but there was some indirect evidence suggesting that such withdrawal did not affect the prosecution of non-domestic violence cases. Similarly, Sanders found that the triviality of non-domestic violence cases did not preclude prosecution. Finally, he came across only one prosecution of domestic violence where the victim was seen by the police as 'undeserving' but several such non-domestic prosecutions.

The key issue according to Sanders, however, was the presence or absence of public disorder. The question was not whether strangers had been assaulted but rather 'when and in what circumstances'. Violence between strangers which did not give rise to public disorder was not treated with the same concern as that which did. However, challenging police authority, even if no public disorder was involved, was likely to lead to a prosecution. Sanders offers a number of explanations as to why public order cases are prosecuted more vigorously. Firstly, there is the obvious point that maintaining order is an essential duty of the police. But there is, Sanders argues, also greater ease of conviction in public order cases. He identifies a number of reasons for this: such cases are tried summarily; victim testimony is unnecessary; and little proof of *mens rea* is required. These factors could well help explain why, when the police do want to arrest in cases of domestic violence, they often, if a public order element is involved, choose to do so not on assault grounds but for breach of the peace, drunkenness and the like thus making the victims' evidence unnecessary.

Sanders' study needs to be replicated with a much larger number of cases before his explanation can be generally accepted. Unfortunately, in Wasoff's (1982) study — which also compared the prosecution of domestic and non-domestic violence cases — the point is not addressed. Indeed, it is unclear whether her sample contained any incidents involving elements of public disorder though it seems probable that it did not since she selected cases reported to three Procurator Fiscal offices in Scotland which "contained an element of violence which might be domestic in origin..." and specifically excluded violent offences associated with theft, traffic offences and offences which had multiple accused. In addition to her analysis of 159 cases (of which just over a third were domestic, mostly wife assaults) she also observed procurators fiscal at work and carried out interviews with them. The procurators chosen for the study represented different career levels, types of work within the fiscal service, and geographical locations.

Wasoff (1982) found no evidence of procurators failing to prosecute because they thought prosecution of domestic violence was inappropriate and might harm family relationships. Decisions not to proceed were based on legal and administrative grounds. This stands in contrast to the work, also in Scotland, of Moody and Tombs (1982) who found that procurators were split between those who saw their role as to mediate to help preserve the marriage and those who thought their task was to prosecute in order to underline the seriousness of the offence. Moreover, although it is often suggested that the need for corroboration — which is often lacking in cases of domestic violence since so much is without witnesses — makes prosecution difficult, Wasoff found no evidence of this posing practical problems for procurators despite many of them stating that it did. (She does, however, note that such problems may have been overcome for them by the police in 'overdetermining' evidence in cases leading to arrest.) As has been discussed earlier, Wasoff also found that claims about 'victims reluctance' were greatly exaggerated. Although the ultimate decision of what charge will be made against the accused lies with the procurator fiscal, Wasoff found that only rarely was the charge presented by the police dropped or changed completely although the wording was sometimes altered. She found that domestic violence tended to be subject to lower charge and was assigned to lower courts than non-domestic cases of equal severity. Wasoff argues that these decisions as to charge and allocation to courts provides evidence of domestic violence cases being treated less seriously than non-domestic violence by the criminal justice system. By contrast, Sanders' (1987) research did not show this.

One final point needs to be considered in relation to the prosecution of domestic violence *viz.* what is the likely impact of the introduction of the Crown Prosecution Service? This has to be a matter of speculation given its recent introduction and there is no research yet available. Two commentators (Edwards, 1985a and 1986d and Sanders, 1987) have, however, voiced the view that it is unlikely to affect matters to any significant extent, though for somewhat different reasons. The Code for Crown Prosecutors provides that all cases should have a realistic prospect of conviction before proceeding. Edwards is of the view that domestic violence has always had a low rate of conviction and, therefore, that crown prosecutors are not likely to proceed with such cases. Sanders, however, says that the police always operated on the principal of a realistic chance of conviction (colloquially referred to as the 51% rule) in domestic cases and, therefore, its formal introduction should not disproportionately affect domestic violence prosecutions. (In fact the Attorney General's Guidelines to the police on prosecution always laid down the reasonable prospect of conviction for *all* cases — the so-called 51% rule.) The reason Sanders believes that the Crown Prosecution Service will not materially affect prosecutions is because those cases which the police decide should not be prosecuted are never brought to their attention. Since the police (and prosecutors) firmly believe that prosecutions fail because of 'victim reluctance', unless there is a major change of policy which helps change police attitudes, it is unlikely that they will take the

65

initial decision to charge and pass domestic violence cases to the Crown Prosecution Service.[1]

The way in which domestic violence was traditionally regarded as intrinsically different from other violent offences and as essentially a family matter led to the belief that criminal prosecution was not a particularly appropriate response and might even cause further damage to the already difficult relationship between the parties. Thus, in North America, in particular, ways were sought to find what was considered a more appropriate forum in which to effect resolution. Often the perceived solution was to give jurisdication to family courts. The best known adoption of the technique is probably in New York where, even if a domestic violence complaint was received in the criminal courts, it was referred to the family court. This is a civil court and the proceedings are in lieu of prosecution. The woman could, in theory, receive an *ex parte* order of protection on the day of her application and a formal temporary order of protection which would remain in effect for up to one year. In practice, however, Dutton (1984) has said that women were first counselled by a probation unit and then a further 60 day period was allowed during which family counselling should take place with a view to reconciliation. During this time, every effort was made to keep the family intact, though if the woman resisted this she could appear before a family court judge. The proceedings of the courts themselves were oriented towards problem solving and the provision of welfare rather than strictly judicial matters (Freeman, 1979) and efforts were made to involve a wide range of social service agencies. In 1977, however, civil and criminal courts were given concurrent jurisdiction over domestic violence offences. Current practice appears to be that the more serious types of assault are directed towards the criminal courts while common assault cases are dealt with by the family courts where the emphasis is still on mediation and counselling (Dutton, 1984).

Family courts do not, of course, exist in Britain although there are pressures for their creation in the hope that they will encourage a less adversarial approach to all family law matters and provide a conciliation (as opposed to reconciliation) service to assist agreement between parties. It is questionable, however, whether domestic violence is appropriate to such a forum. There has been no suggestion of using schemes such as the Bristol Courts Family Conciliation Service for domestic violence cases heard in the criminal courts (Marshall, 1985). As Marshall (1985) has said "there is family conflict and there is family conflict." In some instances, a counselling or social welfare approach may be what is desired by both parties. It is likely that this will be the case where the assault — however reprehensible — is of a minor nature and where there is, to all intents and purposes, still a functioning relationship which some outside help could improve. But in others, matters may have gone so far — the violence may be too severe or have too long a

---

[1] It is worthy of note, however, that in the London Metropolitan Police district, where a new initiative on domestic violence was announced in the summer of 1987, prosecutions of domestic violence rose threefold in the second half of the year compared to the first six months (*The Guardian,* 11 February 1988). Nevertheless, Horley (1988) states that the police have found that the Crown Prosecution Service is reluctant to accept cases of domestic violence.

history — that reconciliation is, in fact, impossible, not desired by the victim and, indeed, potentially dangerous. Mediation techniques rest on there being a compromise solution, and on a common interest in having the matter resolved amicably. But there will be cases of domestic violence where there can be no common interest or compromise because of the severity of the violence or, quite simply, because the victim, whatever the degree of violence endured, feels that mediation is not appropriate. It is suggested that the victims' views are regarded as crucial. They should not be coerced into mediation, counselling or any other form of social welfare if this does not accord with their wishes. Nor should they be given a choice only in theory but, in reality, be pressurised into accepting mediation techniques. To do so would probably fail to be effective since conciliatory counselling is only likely to work where both parties agree with it as a preferred mode of action.

But the overall problem with a predominately counselling approach is that this may become the end in itself and the need to afford protection to the victim can become secondary to the aim of keeping the family intact. Such an approach runs the danger of overlooking the fact that a criminal assault has occurred; it fails to signify that what has happened is a criminal offence for which the full protection of the criminal law, and the agencies which enforce the law, can be and, arguably, should be brought into operation. Non-enforcement of the criminal law can merely add to the belief that domestic violence is somehow or other not really criminal violence. This does not mean that it is necessary to lock up every abuser. Other sentencing options are available and arguably attempts should be made to consider whether available options are sufficient or whether there is a need to try other measures. Counselling and treatment programmes could have a part to play in such a development — a point which will be returned to later in this chapter.

There is some evidence that pro-arrest policies in the United States are bringing changes in prosecutorial practices (Lerman, 1981). There is a move towards specialisation in domestic violence prosecution with domestic violence units being set up in large district attorney departments. These units regularly review police records to identify domestic violence cases. Common 'charging' policies are being developed, and close co-operation is being sought with victim advocates who provide the necessary support to maximise the likelihood of victims co-operating with prosecutors. In some areas, prosecutors have tried to use other corroborating evidence to make their case rather than relying on victim testimony. Some states operate a strict policy against dropping the case to the extent of holding a victim in contempt of court for failure to testify (Herrington, 1986).

Canada, too, has moved towards an enhanced criminal reponse to domestic violence. The police laying charges policy has brought in its wake a number of initiatives to co-ordinate an integrated criminal justice response (see, *inter alia*, MacLeod, 1987; Ontario Standing Committee on Social Development, 1983; and Status of Women, Ottawa, 1986). Included among those are the appointment of specially designated crown attorneys to handle domestic violence cases after specialised training; the employment of part-time assistant crown attorneys to free domestic assault prosecutors at an early stage to help reduce delays in bringing cases to court; the appointment of victim/witness co-ordinators to ensure that the victim has an established contact point during the legal proceedings; the development of victim advocacy services; and the use of victim impact statements. The emphasis is on handling domestic violence in criminal rather than family courts and crown prosecutors are advised that they may accede to requests by a complainant not to proceed only in exceptional cases. Where this happens, the victim is, in general, still put on the witness stand to explain the reasons for her requested withdrawal and to ascertain, so far as possible, that it is not the result of coercion.

There have been similiar developments in Australia where police are now required to lay charges of assault where sufficient evidence exists and prosecutions have to be conducted by a police prosecutor. Moreover, victims have been made compellable witnesses. There is concern, however, at the frequency with which magistrates exempt female victims of domestic violence from giving evidence and consideration is being given as to how best to deal with this (L'orange, 1986).

The practice of some American states of holding women in contempt of court appears unsympathetic to the victim and may add to the trauma already experienced. The value of other developments, however, is less questionable — for example, the shift to placing more reliance upon other evidence of the offence (medical reports, the evidence of the police called to the incident, any witness reports and so on) and less on the victim's testimony. Moreover, the decision to go to court is not an easy one to make. The woman often feels a lack of support and a sense of isolation which is exacerbated by the long delays occurring in court proceedings. Co-operation between prosecutors and victim advocates in the United States and Canada could perhaps be adopted here.

Traditionally domestic violence cases have not met with harsh sentences from the courts. The allocation of domestic violence cases to lower courts observed by Wasoff (1982) has important implications for final disposal since the range of sanctions available is more limited. In the non-domestic cases which were more likely to involve a trial, higher acquittal rates were noted. Again, this stands in contrast to Sanders' (1987) finding that a higher proportion of domestic than non-domestic violence cases ended in acquittal. In examining the disposals made, Wasoff found that, as a group, domestic violence cases had lower fines and shorter prison sentences than non-domestic cases. Fining was by far the common disposal in domestic violence cases (used in more than three quarters of cases) followed by admonition or a deferred sentence on condition of good behaviour and then admonition (16%). Imprisonment was the least frequent outcome (6%). The type of disposals made in non-domestic violence cases was remarkably similar: the difference between the two groups, as mentioned above, lay in the latter receiving higher fines and longer prison sentences. A similar pattern of disposal was found in the Bedfordshire Police study (1976) of domestic violence cases. American research also points to lesser sanctions being imposed for domestic violence compared with violent crime involving strangers (Goolkasian, 1986). Crites (1987) takes the view that, in the United States, traditional judicial responses to domestic violence has "mirrored that found in society at large". She argues that the sentences given to offenders show a tendancy for judges to side with the husband and to be reluctant to view domestic violence as a crime.

Treatment programmes for offenders

It was stated earlier that counselling and treatment programmes could have a part to play in the development of sentencing options which might be thought more appropriate for domestic violence cases.[2] There may be scepticism about programmes which are not sought out be abusers themselves but that scepticism may be misplaced. Only a willingness to experiment and evaluate will tell. It could be, for example, that counselling orders would be taken more seriously if they were made by the criminal courts as part, say, of a probation order.

Treatment programmes for domestic violence abusers are of comparatively recent origin but have grown in number in recent years, particularly in the United States and Canada. There are different models of therapy in operation. Some adopt traditional one-to-one client/therapist approaches; others treat either the couple together or the whole family; and others rely on group therapy techniques for abusers (Browning, 1984; Deschner, 1984; Roy, 1982; Gondolf, 1985a and b; US Law Enforcement Assistance Administration, 1981; Wachtel and Levens, 1984). Most programmes attempt to work on the individual characteristics identified as being associated with wife abuse — problems of self-esteem, depression, alcoholism, poor communication skills and so forth. Gondolf (1984 and 1985) has noted that some go further in attempting to establish 'insight-orineted' techniques and to more broadly resocialise abusers. One of the basic assumptions of the majority of programmes is that violence is a learned behavioural response which, therefore, has to be 'unlearned' by a variety of techniques including emotional awareness, communication training, cognitive restructuring and, in particular, techniques of anger control.[3]

There is little reference in the literature to programmes which are primarily guided by an explanation which roots domestic violence in patriarchal structures and which, therefore, aim to confront sexist attitudes and oppressive behaviours. An exception is those mentioned by Browning (1984) and Gondolf (1984, 1985a and b) for example, the Boston-based EMERGE programme — which, in addition to running anti-sexist training programmes for male abusers, also campaigns to change the traditional responses of the medical profession and criminal justice agencies.

---

[2] A new initiative on domestic violence has recently been announced in Lothian Region, Scotland (*The Scotsman* 15 and 16 February 1988). This involves the close co-operation of the local authority, the police, the procurator fiscal service and Woman's Aid. Counselling and treatment programmes are to be developed on a trial basis for men convicted of domestic violence assaults and the fiscal service has agreed to press for their use instead of fines or imprisonment.

[3] Readers interested in knowing more of the different approaches and methods used should consult Browning, 1984; Currie, 1985; Roy, 1982; Sonkin and Durphy, 1982; and Wachtel and Levens, 1984.

It appears that few wife abusers participate of their own volition in treatment programmes (Martin, 1979; Sinclair 1985). An attempt in New South Wales to encourage abusers to seek help by establishing a telephone crisis link is reported as having met with little success: only 8 telephone calls were received (L'orange, 1986). Increasingly in North America, such programmes are used both as forms of pre-trial diversion and as a sentencing option by the courts (Browning, 1984; Wachtel and Levens, 1984; Herrington, 1986).

Browning (1984) has argued that, until the development of treatment programmes, a crucial deficiency underlying the perceived poor criminal justice response to domestic violence was the lack of workable sentencing options. MacLeod (1987) has noted the view of some counsellors that judges are learning about domestic violence through the existence of treatment counselling programmes and feel that such programmes provide them with more realistic sentencing options. In the words of one counsellor quoted by MacLeod:

> ...Judges also need options so that they can pass fairer sentences. People always talk about changing the attitudes of judges. Well, in my experience, judges are interested when they see a program that can help them pass down a good sentence, and not fill up the jails. Through counselling programs for batterers, judges *ARE* learning about wife-beating.

> [original emphasis]

Sinclair (1985) and MacLeod (1987) both record that such programmes are also viewed positively by women who are victims of domestic violence for they do not, on the whole, wish their partnerships to end but want the violence to stop. Moreover, victims are keener on a criminal justice response, and more willing to co-operate in criminal proceedings, *if* they think their abusers will be treated as a result.

In Australia, the Domestic Violence Committee of the New South Wales Government has suggested that the most appropriate forum for the development of treatment programmes is within the context of the criminal justice system. This indeed may be so but it could perhaps also be the case that any observed changes on the part of court-ordered offenders are likely to be more apparent than real for they know that more punitive sanctions will be brought into force if they do not co-operate in the programmes. It is at least arguable that therapy techniques are only likely to succeed with those who want to change their behaviour and themselves seek treatment. Whilst Wachtel and Levens (1984) — who have monitored the Vancouver programmes which accept court-directed, court-referred and agency-referred abusers — suggest that the threat of other court sanctions — perhaps perceived as less lenient — provides extra leverage and encourages motivation to participate, it may be that the only motivation is to complete the programme, not neccessarily to change.

How much change is effected by such programmes is as yet unknown. The real test has to be that they are actually effective in changing behaviour — in preventing the re-occurrence of domestic violence — not whether or not participants complete the programmes, have improved self-esteem, are less depressive or whatever other measure is used. Gondolf (1985b) and MacLeod (1987) have both pointed to a hidden risk of such programmes commonly voiced by counsellors. There is a fear that participation in treatment may merely help male abusers to express their violence in other, arguably more socially acceptable, ways. In other words, physical violence will simply be replaced by greater use of other forms of cruelty — psychological and verbal violence and increased economic hardship.

Evaluation of treatment programmes to date has been minimal. As yet, there is little clear hard evidence that violence is, in fact, reduced (Gondolf, 1984, 1985b; MacLeod, 1987; Wachtel and Levens, 1984; Wood, 1986). Browning (1984), in his wide-ranging review of Canadian treatment programmes undertaken on behalf of the Federal Department of Health and Welfare, noted that there were "only clinical impressions and loosely-collected self report information support[ing] the contention that men's treatment works". The Department of Health and Welfare in Canada is currently funding research to examine the effectiveness of various treatment programmes but until that becomes available there is almost a dearth of information. An exception is the already mentioned work by Dutton (1986, 1987) who demonstrated — albeit on the basis of a small sample — a greater decrease in recidivism when treatment was appended to arrest. Over a two and a half year follow-up period, 40% of those not participating in a treatment programme were re-arrested; only 4% of those who were so treated were re-arrested. Further support for the effectiveness of treatment is also found in the work of Edeleson and Gruszinski (forthcoming, quoted in Dutton, 1987). Although these results may be encouraging, Dutton (1987) warns that they should be regarded as tentative until other, larger-scale, studies have been completed. Nevertheless, this need not inhibit the development of programmes here on an experimental basis, subject to evaluation. It is unlikely that any one form of therapy will suit all offenders and again there is a need to experiment. Furthermore, it is important that evaluations are conducted of effectiveness over time.

9 Seeking help outside the criminal justice system

There are many agencies outside the criminal justice system which ought to be in a position of affording help to victims of domestic violence. They include friends and family networks, the medical profession, social services departments, lawyers, housing aid centres, women's organisations and the refuge movement. The question examined in this chapter is the extent to which they provide that help and how effective they are.

Friends and family

Most research which has examined help-seeking behaviour has noted that there is a marked reluctance to seek any help after the first experience of a domestic violence attack (see, for example, Bowker, 1983; Dobash and Dobash, 1979; Dobash *et al.*, 1985; Pahl, 1985). A variety of reasons are presented for this but most research shows that the most inhibiting factor is that a sense of shame is experienced by victims. Women are ashamed to tell outsiders what has happened to them and their marriage. They may believe the assault to be a unique event. In some cases they are intimidated by threats of further violence if they tell anyone. But there is also a fear that they will be blamed for causing the attack by not being a 'good wife'. However, as the violence continues and increases, although the inhibiting factors still remain, help is, indeed, sought. The Dobash research team (1985) found that this was increasingly the case. After the first attack only about half of the 109 women they interviewed sought outside help, whereas 88% sought help after the worst attack and almost all (97%) did after the last attack before they left their husbands. Almost all women turn at first to families and friends and only as the violence continues do they seek help from more formal agencies whilst continuing to use family networks (Carlson, 1977; Dobash *et al.*, 1985; Binney *et al.*, 1981; Flynn, 1977; Pahl, 1985).

In the beginning, help is sought not to break up the marriage but to stop the violence. There is a need for emotional support, a sympathetic ear. As the violence fails to end, the need for help becomes more directly concerned with practical help and assistance. Pahl (1985) also notes that friends again become very important at a much later stage, after victims have taken the decision to leave and are trying to re-establish a life for themselves.

The medical profession

In many cases of domestic violence, the medical profession, and especially general practioners, is the first formal agency to which victims turn for help. Most research

72

has had to rely on accounts given by the women themselves since problems of confidentiality usually preclude approaching doctors direct. A notable exception is the work by Borkowski *et al.* (1983) who interviewed 50 general practioners. Time precluded their undertaking a systematic search of their medical records; instead doctors provided rough estimates of how often they were consulted on problems of marital violence. These estimates suggest that, given the large numbers of patients seen overall, cases of marital violence were encountered only infrequently. More than four fifths of the doctors thought they would be consulted by a female victim at least every six months: interestingly, just over a quarter of doctors thought they would be consulted by a male victim within the same timescale.

Studies relying on the responses of samples of female victims of domestic violence have produced varying estimates of the extent to which they seek help from doctors. American research tends to show lower rates than British research but this may be a function of the privatised nature of medicine in the USA. Pagelow's (1981a) study of 157 battered women, for example, showed that less than half had consulted a doctor although two thirds said they needed medical attention but had not sought it for a number of reasons. The most common reason was that their spouses forbade it, threatening further violence if they did. In this country, Dobash and Dobash's (1979) interviews with 109 women living in refuge houses revealed that four fifths had consulted a doctor at some point but only for very few (3%) of all the violent attacks they had experienced. Pahl's (1979) interviews with 50 battered women showed that about two thirds had consulted their GPs about the violence in their marriage whilst Binney *et al.* (1981) put the figure at just over half of their sample of 656 (again this comprised women living in refuges).

It appears, however, that having sufficiently overcome feelings of shame and fears of reprisal by their spouses to visit their GPs women, once there, find it difficult to approach the subject of domestic violence directly. Again feelings of shame seemed to prevent them making direct admissions of the causes of their injuries. This has been noted by both Pahl (1979) (no figures given) and Dobash and Dobash (1979) who estimated that only a quarter of women seeking medical help actually revealed that they had been beaten. Instead, they either fabricated explanations or only hinted at problems in the hope that the doctor would bring the matter out openly, thus relieving them of the necessity for doing so. The Dobashes' study, however, — in common with that of Nuttall *et al.* (1985) in Canada — revealed that this happened rarely; doctors usually remained non-committal, treating the medical symptoms but offering little other help or assistance by way of referral to non-medical agencies. Where advice was offered, it usually took the form of advising the woman to leave. It seems from the work of Borkowski *et al.* (1983) that many GPs do not see it as appropriate for them to be concerned with marital problems which manifest themselves in violence except in fulfilling the traditional role of treating injuries and illnesses — 'real medicine'. The prescription of tranquillizers and/or referrals of victims to psychiatrists appears to be a frequent part of the treatment given (Walker, 1979; Stark *et al.*, 1979; Dobash *et al.*, 1985; Dobash and Dobash, 1979; Pahl, 1979; Binney *et al.*, 1981; Borkowski *et al.*, 1983).

73

If only a little is known about the response of general practitioners, even less is known about accident and emergency departments, though given the relative anonymity they provide — and also their 24 hour access — they may be a popular source of help to the victim of domestic violence. No reliable figures are available as to how often they are used. An attempt to estimate the number of domestic violence cases dealt with in Bristol (Borkowski *et al.*, 1983) revealed a monthly average of two cases in each of two large general hospitals; the maximum cases reported in any one month was six. The research team themselves, however, noted that their data collection system was not 'foolproof' and recorded instances where they knew of cases which never appeared in their data. Walker's (1979) experience in the United States suggests that domestic violence goes unrecorded by doctors in emergency departments simply because they have no time to probe or question the reason why injuries have been sustained. Stark *et al.* (1979) — also in the United States — have, however, offered a somewhat different view in that they believe that emergency room staff not only systematically ignore the causes of battered women's injuries, but also seek to shift the responsibility for them on to the women themselves and encourage them to define the assault as a 'family matter'. They analysed the medical records of 481 women who sought aid for injuries at a major urban hospital emergency room during a period of one month and concluded that the number of battered women using the service was ten times higher than that estimated by physicians.

Although, as Pahl has noted (1982b), health visitors' responsibilities, in theory at least, extend to the whole community within which they work, it appears that they are an under-used source of assistance. Binney *et al.* (1981) found that less than a quarter of their sample had contacted health visitors whilst Borkowski *et al.*'s (1983) survey of community agencies found that battered women comprised just under 2% of health visitors' caseloads. In both Pahl's (1985) and Binney *et al.*'s (1981) studies, health visitors were found to be primarily concerned with the welfare of any children and thus attached importance to keeping the family together.

The medical profession could play a crucial role in helping domestic violence victims. As has been stated above, they are often the first formal agency to whom victims turn for help. By being more knowledgeable about sources of help, being prepared to acknowledge the existence of domestic violence, probing to discover its existence and, above all, being willing to accept a more widely defined role and responsibilities, they could ensure that victims know where to go for help and actually make referrals for them in appropriate cases. Another possible role for the general practitioner is to keep careful records of the injuries sustained (including their type and severity) which might then be used as evidence in court should the need arise. This, too, would also require a more inquiring attitude (than currently appears to exist) as to how the injuries came about. Health visitors could also contribute in many ways. Domestic violence often starts or increases during pregnancy, the time when women see health visitors routinely. Moreover, given that some women are deterred, if not prevented, from visiting their GPs by threats of further retaliatory violence, the home visits of health visitors provide an opportunity to seek and receive advice.

Social services

It is important to recognise that local authority social services departments do not have statutory responsibility for domestic violence victims. Any involvement with them is, therefore, likely to come about as a result of intervention with families on other grounds. It appears that victims themselves do not have any clear idea of the assistance social services departments can provide and that such departments are not immediately thought of as a source of help (Dobash and Dobash, 1979). Nevertheless, Dobash and Dobash found that three quarters of their sample of women had contacted social workers at least once during the violent relationship. Although very few (5%) of the contacts made after the first attack were with social workers, after the last attack, prior to leaving the relationship, this had risen to almost a fifth — the largest single category of contacts made (Dobash *et al.*, 1985). Bowker (1983) also noted a rise in social service contacts from the first attack (7% of women) to the last (43% of women). In Pahl's study (1985) three quarters of the 42 women she interviewed had contacted social workers prior to entering a refuge and much the same proportion also sought their help on leaving it and trying to establish a new life.

It is difficult to estimate what proportion of social workers' caseloads are concerned with domestic violence. Since some of the contacts come about as a result of other involvement, it is difficult to identify domestic violence cases since these will often be 'hidden' under some other classification. Borkowski *et al.* (1983) have suggested a figure of 12.5% but this is based on social workers' own estimates. Maynard (1985), using a different method of analysis (she had access to case records), estimated that domestic violence was involved in about one third of cases. (She drew a one in ten random sample of all current files in a town in the north of England; this yielded 103 cases for analysis.) This was in marked contrast to the advice that she had received form social workers that she would find only one or two cases. Both Borkowski *et al.* and Maynard suggest that their figures are substantial underestimates.

In Maynard's (1985) study, the vast majority of files indicated that nothing was immediately done to help the victim. Instead, there was a marked tendency to redefine the problem as a matter of concern for child welfare rather than domestic violence *per se*. Against this, Binney *et al.* (1981) and Pahl (1985) found that social workers were by far the most common source of referral to refuges. Bowker's (1983) American study showed that the most common response of social workers was to 'talk about the problem'. Actual practical assistance and suggestions about problem solving occurred only infrequently. In this country the Dobash research team (1985) also found that supportive assistance in the form of providing a sympathetic ear was the most common response.

What emerges from all the studies is a concern on the part of social workers to keep families together, to stress the need for reconciliation and to put the interests of children first. Dobash and Dobash (1979), for example, found that social workers only acted quickly to assist women practically or to suggest separation when they

75

perceived children as being in physical danger. Moreover, they also record instances where social workers threatened to remove children from their mothers, especially where women had made a break from their husbands but had failed to find accommodation regarded as of adequate standard. The threat of losing their children can be sufficient for women to return to the family home and to a recurrence of the violence they had experienced. This paramount concern with family reconciliation may stem in part from social workers' basic training which stresses working within the family context to solve problems occurring in families. Maynard (1985), however, also found examples from the files she studied where women were implicitly and explicitly blamed for the violence they endured. Thus domestic failings either in terms of housekeeping abilities or "failing to meet sexual demands", although not regarded as a legitimate reason for violence, were nevertheless regarded by social workers as "understandable": an "almost rational response to certain failings on the woman's part". Maynard also found examples on the files of explicit blame: "It seems her nagging is the trigger for his violence". Moreover, there was also evidence that social workers disbelieved the women's account of violence whilst at the same time recorded the details. As Maynard noted, social workers' behaviour was largely determined by underlying attitudes of women's role as wives and mothers and not as individuals, by their images of women who are victims of domestic violence and their beliefs as to why violence occurs.

Social workers ought to be in a powerful position to aid domestic violence victims. The training they receive in interpersonal skills compared to that received by the police, for example, should, arguably, make them better equipped to attempt crisis intervention in a meaningful way. Yet it appears that there is a marked reluctance to adopt such an active role. This is not to argue that crisis intervention should be the appropriate response — or, more particularly, the only response — to domestic violence. There may be stages in the development of violence between spouses where it is appropriate and others where it is not. However, when women begin to seek help they are usually seeking help not to effect a break in the relationship but to get the violence to stop. It also seems the case that, at least in the early stages of violence, assailants do experience remorse. This may well be the time at which crisis intervention skills and counselling of both parties would have a greater chance of success. This would require not only that women seek help at the first sign of violence but also that there would be a willingness on the part of agencies whose help is sought to respond positively at such an early stage and, crucially, a willingness on the part of the women's spouses to participate. What seems to happen, however, is that action comes too late: only when matters have deteriorated to a great extent and violence has grown very severe and escalated in frequency does it seem that any real response is forthcoming. By then, counselling techniques and family reconciliation have less chance of success. Indeed, it could be argued that by that point they would be totally inappropriate and could even force victims back into relationships of extreme personal danger.

Women's Aid and the provision of refuge accommodation

The ideology of women's refuges stands in marked contrast to that of social work departments. Conciliation, keeping families intact and 'care-taking' is not their goal. Their first aim is to provide women with a means of physical escape from situations *they* find intolerable. A key part of the philosophy is that it is for victims themselves to make their own definition of what is intolerable and their own judgement as to when they need to leave and seek shelter. The emphasis is very much on developing self-help in the women who go to shelters, encouraging them to take control of their lives and make their own decisions (for example, whether or not to return home or to establish a new life on their own or with their children). Additionally, the Women's Aid Federation (England) — founded in 1975 from the local groups which set up shelters — also includes within its formal aims:

> To educate and inform the public, the media, the police, the courts, the social services and other authorities with respect to the battering of women, mindful of the fact that this is a result of the general position of women in society.

The Women's Aid Federation (England) is the only national voluntary organisation dealing solely with violence against women: the major part of its income is provided by a central government grant — currently about £100,000 per annum. Its role is to co-ordinate the work of local groups and to provide information and advice to local refuges in addition to its information and campaigning functions.

The first, and perhaps still the best known, refuge to be established was that in Chiswick in 1971. By 1975, 30 had been established and, by 1978 — the date of the Department of the Environment's funded survey of refuge accommodation undertaken by Binney *et al.* (1981) — there were 150 in existence. This was only one sixth of the level of provision recommended by the Select Committee in 1975 which had advocated that there should be an *initial* target of one family place (ie for a woman and her children) per 100,000 of the population. Moreover, Binney *et al.* (1981) found that there was uneven distribution of refuge provision over the country as a whole. By 1987 the number of refuges had risen to just over 200.

A consistent problem noted in the research literature concerns the inadequate funding of refuges (see Binney *et al.*, 1981; Clifton, 1985; Wilson, 1983). Local refuges had sometimes obtained financial help for paid workers from the Manpower Services Commission or from Urban Aid. By 1985, however, Binney *et al.* (1985) noted that the former source had virtually disappeared, whilst the latter was limited to certain areas. During the financial year 1985/86 almost £100,000 was provided under the Urban Aid Programme to some 57 refuges. Estimates of the need for refuges and their financial provision are essentially a matter for local authorities who may fulfil this need themselves or in partnership with a voluntary organisation. However, research has shown that it has often proved difficult for refuges to obtain help from local authority departments. Thus, in 1978, Binney *et al.* found that only 10% of refuges received any money from local authority housing departments and the average amount received was just under £800. Despite the duties imposed on local authorities by the *Housing Act 1985*, many housing departments have refused to provide groups with suitable properties to set up refuges. Reliance, instead, has been placed upon the provision of bed and breakfast accommodation. Yet Binney *et al.* (1985) argue that refuges are a cheaper and more suitable form of accommodation. Where housing was provided, both Binney *et al.* (1985) and Clifton (1985) have noted that this was generally of poor quality and that local authorities have poor maintenance records. The poor conditions are said to be exacerbated by the overcrowding prevalent in all refuges.

There is evidence from both Canada and Australia of a growing importance and commitment to the role of the refuge movement as a means of coping with domestic violence. In New South Wales in Australia, for example, there are now 46 women's refuges funded at a rate of $9 million dollars per annum through the Commonwealth/State supported Accommodation Assistance Programme (L'orange 1986). In Canada, between 1979 and 1985, the number of refuges increased by 300% to 250, the primary method of funding is under welfare/social services or assisted housing programmes at local level. Ways are being sought to expand the services offered by shelters by making links with other available and appropriate services and by assisting refuge residents in seeking access to these services (Wood, 1986).

Binney *et al.* (1981) note that:

> Despite the appalling conditions and overcrowding in many refuges, the women interviewed talked very positively about their experience of living there.

The importance of shelters lies not just in their provision of temporary emergency accommodation which provides a necessary means of escape from a violent home. Although most victims turn to families and friends for help, many do not have such networks but are socially isolated. In Pahl's (1985) study almost a quarter of the women were in this position. For them, the existence of shelters is perhaps of special importance. But for all who seek refuge there is, in addition to the protection and the practical help and assistance provided, emotional support which helps overcome the common feelings of isolation and aids a growing self-confidence (Clifton, 1985). The psychological effects of domestic violence — the learned helplessness discussed earlier — begin to be overcome though it may be a long and difficult process. Thus two thirds of Binney *et al.*'s (1981) sample claimed improved personal mental health after moving to a refuge. Moreover, they further claimed improvement in their children's physical and mental health. One of the perceived beneficial features of refuge life was the existence of a social network of women who had a common experience of domestic violence. The emotional support given by that network helps to restore confidence. Moreover, it appears that support often continues after the women have left the refuge and while they are in need of help as they struggle to re-establish their lives.

The length of time spent in refuges varies greatly between individuals. Some stay only a few days, others several months (Binney *et al.* 1981; Pahl, 1985). Although some studies have shown that a considerable proportion of women return to their husbands, others do not. Statistics from Welsh Women's Aid (1980) and Scottish Women's Aid (1980) suggest that approximately two fifths do return. However, these statistics are based on what women do *immediately* on leaving the refuge.

Studies which look at patterns of behaviour over a longer time scale — for example, Pahl (1985) and Binney *et al.* (1981) — show that, in the longterm, most women do leave their spouses. In Pahl's study, almost half never returned to their husbands and, of those who did, only a fifth were still with their husbands after two years. She found them, however, "unenthusiastic about their married lives". Binney *et al.*'s (1981) larger study showed that only 14% returned to their husbands from the refuge; at the second interview stage, only 11% were with their husbands. Again they found that "the majority of the women were still very unhappy".

10 Victims' satisfaction with help received

A number of studies have examined victims' satisfaction with the response they received to requests for assistance. One of the problems of these studies is that it is not always clear exactly what response was desired on any one occasion and by what criteria 'helpfulness' or 'satisfaction' was being judged. Requests for support are generally addressed to families and friends though also to GPs (who, of course, are asked to treat injuries) whilst the police, in particular (but to some extent, too, other agencies, especially social workers) are expected to intervene to help stop the violence.

Family and friends

Within the family, it is to mothers and sisters that women most usually turn for help (Bowker, 1983; Pahl, 1985) though the help of both parents is more commonly sought than that of friends (Dobash and Dobash, 1979). Pahl found that almost three fifths of siblings but just under half of parents were regarded as helpful. The Dobashes' (1979) research in this country found that providing 'a sympathetic ear' was almost always forthcoming from families but that requests for more specific help, for example, for accommodation, were not automatically met. In some cases for example — although not many — such requests were refused. Most who provided accommodation did so on the understanding that it was to be on a temporary basis. This stands in contrast to Bowker's American study which showed direct help in the form of material aid (accommodation and money) was the most common response from families (50%) and the provision of 'a sympathetic ear' was the least common response (5%). The differences observed between the two studies may be due to variations in the composition of their samples. In the Scottish study, almost all of the 109 women interviewed came from working class families and all had sought refuge in a shelter. In Bowker's study, however, three tenths of the 136 women interviewed had family backgrounds which were either professional or managerial and just under a third were from 'blue collar' or working class backgrounds. Presumably, therefore, the families in Bowker's study were better placed to offer material assistance.

Direct confrontation of the husband with his violence by family members occurred only rarely in both Bowker's and the Dobashes' samples. The latter explain this (providing examples) as stemming from the view that what goes on in a marriage is a private matter in which, even if requested by their daughter, parents should not intervene. Dobash and Dobash (1979) also record that counter-assault upon the husband, whether by relatives or friends, was extremely rare but could in fact provide a salutary lesson. In a few cases, they say it has a "startling effect" by making husbands scared, teaching them what it was like to be a victim and by showing that others might come to the defence of their partners. Bowker (1983) records no instances of counter-assault and, indeed, found a few cases of violence which actually occurred in front of family members who made no effort to stop it.

Pahl (1985) and Bowker (1983) record a very high level of satisfaction with the help accorded by friends, higher than that expressed for family members. Pahl's study was conducted over a relatively long time-scale and followed the experiences of women seeking shelter in a refuge from within a few days of arrival there to a final interview two years later. She found that the importance of friends grew over that time and that friends proved to be the most important source of help in attempts to establish a new life. Thus, prior to coming to the refuge, three quarters of Pahl's sample said friends were helpful but after the stay in the refuge, almost all (93%) said this was the case. The great majority of friends were female. Some had been friends over many years, but a great many of those providing help in establishing a new life were, in fact, women with whom they had become friends during their stay in the refuge or whom they had met through organisations for single parents such as Gingerbread. The help given by Gingerbread was also rated highly by the sample of women in the Binney et al. (1981) study who knew of its existence, but the number who did so was, in fact, very small (4% of the sample). This points to the need for better information on such self-help groups being available.

Dobash and Dobash (1979) distinguish between neighbours who are friends and neighbours who remain just that, neighbours. In general, they found that neighbours who were not friends were unsupportive, distant and unlikely to intervene even to the extent of calling the police when they heard or witnessed an assault: the most common response was to pretend it was not happening and to do nothing. In some cases, however, indifference gave way to open hostility — verbal abuse and taunting the victim. Although Bowker (1983) distinguishes friends from neighbours, it is not clear whether he includes in the latter neighbours who are also friends. If he does, then this may explain why his findings do not consistently bear out those of Dobash and Dobash (1979). He found, for example, that instances of neighbours being apathetic and unhelpful were more than balanced by instances of help being received. Since some of the help he records includes providing emergency shelter and refuge and calling the police at a pre-arranged signal, it does seem probable that his definition of neighbour also embraces friends who are neighbours.

General practitioners

In Pahl's study (1985), just over two fifths of the women who had consulted a doctor prior to coming to the refuge had found them helpful. (No comparable figures are given for the follow-up period.) Helpfulness in Pahl's study was seen as a willingness to listen, a sympathetic attitude, and the provision of advice both of a medical and non-medical nature. Binney et al. (1981) put the level of satisfaction higher (56%). In order to give help, however, there has to be knowledge of what sources of help are available and the Borkowski et al. study (1983) seems to suggest that such knowledge is scant. Dobash and Dobash (1979) also note that women want doctors to provide them with the opportunity to talk about their problems and to have them listened to and are grateful when this occurs, even if no other advice or assistance is offered. They record a few instances where doctors went out of their way to help the woman to the extent of trying to reason with the husband and convince him that the violence should stop. However, these were the exceptional cases. The work of Binney *et al.* (1981) and Pahl (1979) points to the dissatisfaction of women with general practitioners who rely upon the prescription of tranquillizers as a response to help. This was mentioned in both studies by women who did not find their doctors helpful. Tranquillizers were seen as inappropriate, stop-gap measures which only served to postpone long term solutions. Dobash and Dobash (1979), however, found a diverse range of attitudes towards the use of drugs: some women felt they could not do without them whereas others thought doctors relied upon them as an alternative to dealing with the real problem.

The legal profession

In Pahl's survey (1985) solicitors were consistently found to be very helpful at both interview stages: just over three quarters of the women expressed satisfaction. It may well be, however, that such satisfaction is a function of the precise roles solicitors were asked to play in regard to domestic violence and the fact that they have the necessary expertise to fulfil that function. Bowker (1983) does not distinguish between lawyers and district attorneys in his examination of victims' satisfaction with the legal profession. He, too, records that there is a fairly high level of satisfaction expressed (60%) but notes that there were, however, many reported negative incidents, especially of district attorneys who often urged women to drop charges or refused to act in any way other than to informally warn the victim's husband.

Social services

Binney *et al.* (1981) found half the women in their sample had at some time sought help from social services departments, and, of those, more than half had found that contact useful. This is very similar to Pahl's (1985) finding at the time of first interview and to Bowker's (1983) American study. Pahl notes that this satisfaction was often due to social workers having been personally responsible for their arrival at the refuge. However, by the time of the second interview, about three quarters of those who had contacted a social worker in the intervening period had found them helpful. Pahl records that the type of help needed changed between the two interviews. At the first stage, what was immediately important to the women was obtaining accurate information, finding accommodation and, in particular, learning of the existence of a refuge. By the time of the second interview, however, most women were predominantly concerned with making a new home and the problems of life as a single parent. What was most valued in the help given by social workers at this point was their ability to 'work the system' on their behalf. This involved social workers not merely advising on what services were available, and from whom, but actively assuming a negotiating role on behalf of the women with other relevant departments within local authorities. They were thus instrumental in obtaining local authority housing, securing housing repairs, arranging childcare facilities and also in obtaining furniture, bedding and cooking equipment. Their knowledge of legislation affecting domestic violence victims was found to be most helpful. Pahl observes that the differences in satisfaction are between the woman living on her own and the woman still living with her husband. Many women had been in need of detailed advice and active support for years before taking the decision to leave and go to a shelter. Yet that advice had not been readily forthcoming and was often limited to being urged to keep the family intact. However, as soon as the victim left, Pahl contends that she is redefined as being on her own and, therefore, both in need and deserving of help and assistance.

In addition to analysing women's satisfaction with social workers' response, Pahl (1985) also provides information on how the help given by social security officials was rated. Again she found a marked difference between the two interview stages but, in the case of social security staff, the very high satisfaction expressed at the earlier stage — more than three quarters — dropped dramatically by the time of the second interview to less than half. It is noteworthy that this was the agency consulted by nearly all women at both interview stages. Pahl attributes the initial high satisfaction as at least partly due to the very low expectations women had. Some, for example, had no awareness of any entitlements they might have to benefits and were only too grateful for any financial help they received. By the time of the second interview, however — when just over a fifth were still supported entirely by supplementary benefit — they had become more knowledgeable about the benefits to which they were entitled. Common criticisms made at this later stage were that errors were often made in payments, that there was little by way of explanation as to the basis on which decisions were made, and that they were not informed what their entitlements were but had to find this out for themselves. All of the women who were living entirely on supplementary benefit expressed a desire to be in paid employment, but lack of child care facilities precluded it. Pahl notes that all of those who had either managed to make child care provisions or whose children were older and less in need of constant care, took jobs as soon as they became available and preferred even unpleasant and low-paid work to being dependent on state benefits.

The police

Given the criticisms made in the research literature of police actions — or non-actions — regarding incidents of domestic violence, it is not surprising that the level of satisfaction with police responses tends to be low in comparison with that of other agencies. Bowker (1982), for example, found that lawyers, district attorneys, social service agencies and clergy all received higher success ratings. In this country, Pahl's (1982a, 1985) study showed that, at the time of first interview, least satisfaction was expressed with police services — just over a third finding them helpful — in comparison to the help provided by family, friends and neighbours, general practitioners, social workers, health visitors, social security officials and solicitors. This figure is very similar to the findings of Binney et al. (1981).

The criteria used to evaluate helpfulness and usefulness are only infrequently made explicit. This makes it difficult to compare studies or to draw firm conclusions. Both Kennedy and Homant's (1983) and Brown's (1984) studies in the United States, for example, found that approximately 70% of women found the police to be 'at least a little helpful' (in Kennedy and Homant's study) and either 'concerned *and* helpful' or 'concerned but *not* helpful' (Brown's study). Quite what is being measured is difficult to unravel. In contrast, Bowker (1983) found that the women in his sample found the police to be successful in about a third of incidents. Pagelow (1981) records that only a third of women in her sample who had called the police regarded their attitude and behaviour favourably.

In Pahl's study (1982a, 1985) those who thought the police had been helpful did so largely because the police had advised them of the existence of the refuge. Unhelpfulness was characterised as a reluctance to intervene in anything other than a minimal way, a reluctance to arrest even when asked to do so and a similar reluctance even in cases where the severity of injuries sustained would seem to have supported an arrest. It also appeared that several of the women who found the police unhelpful thought that the police emphasis upon reconciliation was inappropriate to the circumstances: that matters had reached a point where protection was required. Finally, it also appears that advice was rarely offered to these women regarding legal proceedings and, where given, was unsatisfactory and inadequate.

Satisfaction with the police, however, rose sharply between Pahl's (1985) first and second interviews. At the later stage, half of the women had needed police help during the intervening period, usually to enforce an injunction or to give protection during a reconciliation attempt. These women found the police now more likely to take action and four fifths expressed satisfaction with the police. Indeed, at the time of the second interview, only friends and neighbours were regarded as more helpful (Pahl, 1985). Pahl ascribes these differences to the same reasons as she does the change in social workers' actions and consequent satisfaction levels expressed about them. She argues that it is when women actually leave their partners that the police will readily intervene to help them in a tangible way. Until then, there is a reluctance to become involved in what is regarded as a private matter. Binney *et al.* (1981), however, found no such change in satisfaction with the police. The women in their sample criticised the placatory role still adopted by the police even after they had separated from their husbands.

It is worthy of note that in Jaffe *et al.*'s (1986c) Canadian study dissatisfaction with the police fell sharply after the introduction of the laying charges policy. In 1979 (pre-policy change) almost half of Jaffe *et al.*'s sample of victims were dissatisfied with the police: in 1983, two years after the policy change, only 5% were dissatisfied with the response from police officers.

Refuges and women's groups

Refuges appear to be successful in providing for the needs of women who are the victims of domestic violence. Despite criticisms of the adequacy of accommodation provided, Binney *et al.* (1985) report that the women they interviewed "talked very positively about about their experience of living there''. Clifton (1985), too, states that refuges provide women with far more than accommodation in a crisis. The total experience of living there as part of a community, the members of which had common histories of violence, was highly valued. The high regard for refuges has also been noted in Canada (Ontario Status of Women Council, 1980) where it has been said that, according to women themselves, they are the *only* agency which manages to meet their needs. Finally, Bowker (1983) records that those women in his sample who had help from women's groups spoke of their experience ''in glowing terms''.

Common themes, common responses

Earlier in this review, the attitudes underlying police responses to domestic violence were examined. Reluctance to intervene was, to a large part, shaped by notions and assumptions about the role of women in society and, in particular, within families as wives and mothers; the importance attached to 'family life' and the consequent perceived need for families to stay intact; and the privacy traditionally accorded families in which state intervention is seen as being mainly inappropriate unless it is designed to help families stay together.

From the above examination of the responses of other agencies, it is apparent that these attitudes shape not only police responses but underpin those of other agencies and also those of family and friends. Many pieces of research have commented on the importance of the privacy of the home and the sanctity of marriage. Borkowski *et al.*'s (1983) survey of community agencies, for example, led them to conclude that privacy was a central issue. Agencies might differ to some extent in the importance they attached to it, but it was a concept important to all, a concept which helped determine the patterning of their responses. Pahl's edited collection (1985) also attests to the importance of privacy and ideological notions of the family. In line with other studies — save perhaps Sanders (1987) small scale study of the prosecution process which identified public disorder as a decisive factor — it points to violence being, if not exactly ignored, minimised *because* it takes place within the family home. Readiness to give help and assistance was more apparent — at least in Pahl's (1985) study although not in Binney *et al.*'s (1981) — once the woman had made the break from home. There was then a greater willingness to define the woman as being in need and as deserving of help.

But the importance attached to marriage and to keeping families together is also strong among female domestic violence victims themselves. Typically, they do not leave after their experience of domestic violence and they endure it for many years before accepting that it will not stop. The importance they also attach to the privacy of family life can, for a while, inhibit them from seeking help. When they do, the pattern of help-seeking is such that at first they rely upon families and friends or general practitioners who are more likely to keep the knowledge 'private'. It is only with reluctance that they involve more formal agencies and make public their private predicament.

The respect afforded the privacy of family life can and does inhibit any attempts to deal with the problem. Pahl (1985) suggests that:

> ...conceptions of privacy can militate against both short term and long term solutions...

Borkowski *et al.* (1985) make the same point somewhat differently:

> The irony is that privacy contributes to, and reinforces, the intimacy and sense of solidarity in family life that society values, while it also nurtures and protects the very conditions in which conflict and violence develop.

If the respect afforded the privacy of the family is at the expense of the respect afforded individuals' rights within it, then the question arises whether or not that is too high a cost to be paid. As Faragher (1985) has put it:

> Whose privacy? Whose liberty?

'Blaming the victim' was also discerned as a police response. This, too, was a feature of some other agencies' responses. It was implicit in the referrals made by general practitioners to psychiatrists (see, for example, Dobash and Dobash, 1979) described in a number of studies but it was quite explicit in Maynard's (1985) study of social workers' case notes. Blaming the victim is also implicit in the often posed question: 'why doesn't she leave?' — the argument is that if the woman was blameless, then she would. But the question is too simplistic. It overlooks the complex nature of commitment within relationships. The decision to leave is not unproblematic: there are many hurdles to be overcome. At least in the early stages, victims may cling to the belief that their assailants will change and the violence will end (see Gelles, 1976 but cf. Pagelow 1981b). The psychological effects women experience as a result of violence can often render them incapable of taking the necessary steps to end the relationship. Women with children often stay in the belief that this will be better for the child's welfare. If a woman has nowhere to go, she is faced with the dilemma of leaving her children behind or running the risk of having them taken into care. If she takes them with her, then she knows they will, in all probability, suffer economic hardship as she herself is likely to do. If she has sought help and found little or none forthcoming, this may act as a deterrent to her leaving by increasing her sense of isolation and powerlessness. Most research indicates, however, that if viable alternatives are available — especially access to accommodation — and if there is the necessary support and encouragement, most women will try to take steps to leave.

11 Future directions? A discussion

It would be difficult to disagree with the conclusion of the Women's National Commission (1985) that:

> . . . failure to tackle domestic violence devalues individuals and undermines society.

Whatever the methodological difficulties involved in attempts to estimate the extent of domestic violence — and such difficulties are considerable — all the evidence points to the existence of a potentially very large problem, a problem which does not necessarily become public frequently and, even when it does, is often trivialised, if not ignored. The violence which is endured in the home is often of a very severe nature involving serious physical injury and resulting in psychological and emotional damage to the victims who are, in the main, women. Domestic violence is not a new phenomenon but has a very long history. It has been practised throughout the ages and at times such practice has been not only socially condoned but also upheld by the law. It would be tempting to argue that little has changed over the course of time, but that would be simplistic. The law no longer — at least explicitly — lends its support to wife-beating. The criminal law — with the exception of marital rape — theoretically, treats domestic assaults as it does any other form of assault. The civil law measures passed in the 1970s promised much in the way of legal and practical assistance to victims. But the infrequent enforcement of the criminal law and the restrictive interpretation of civil law provisions suggests an ambivalence towards such behaviour.

However, it is not just the law and its agents who enforce and apply it and who, by their actions, fail to condemn domestic violence whole-heartedly. The studies reviewed here of other agencies — social services, different branches of the medical profession, local authority housing departments and so on — all point in the same direction; domestic violence is condoned up to certain limits. It is only when it exceeds those limits that condemnation becomes overt. What those limits are, however, may have become more problematic than the old notion of the 'rule of thumb'. In the absence of research in this country, it is difficult to be certain what degree of normative support for domestic violence exists in society, though the research by Dobash and Dobash (1979) on the reaction of family and friends suggests that it might be widespread. It seems hardly likely that the attitudes and beliefs which underpin agencies' reactions are not merely a reflection of wider societal attitudes and beliefs. In the United States, Greenblat (1985), in an aptly titled article 'Don't beat your wife . . . unless', has demonstrated that, despite expressions of condemnation in the abstract, there are certain situations in which domestic violence is seen as almost a legitimate response to different types of behavioural patterns by the victim. Admittedly, Greenblat's study was based on a small student sample which might not be representative of the more general population. Arguably, however, it might be expected that students would have more 'progressive' or 'liberal' attitudes. However, only about one tenth of Greenblat's 124 respondents disapproved of all domestic violence whatever the circumstances leading up to it.

There is no easy answer to the question 'what can be done?' It is unlikely that there is one answer or solution. Instead, the nature of the problem suggests that it has to be tackled on a number of fronts. The victim of domestic violence has been identified as having many needs which have to be addressed in order to provide short and long term relief. There is the obvious need that victims require immediate protection from violence. It is here that the police have the greatest role to play, but research has suggested that often their role is limited to talking to the couple and then leaving the scene. This may well add to the feelings of isolation experienced by victims. Further, it may foster the belief that no-one will help and that there is, therefore, no solution. There is likely to be a need for medical attention to treat the injuries. But research also shows that the damage inflicted is not limited to physical injury. There can be considerable psychological damage to the extent that battered women experience a type of paralysis induced by fear so that they are incapable of doing anything about their situation. Self-blame is also a common response leading to feelings of worthlessness. Counselling by professional staff or trained volunteers may help victims to overcome such psychological damage.

For women who decide that the only solution is to leave the marital home, there is a need for suitable accommodation. Often this means looking to the community for help. This is often provided in refuges, but they can provide only temporary relief and permanent housing has to be found. Most women are still in a position of economic dependency which often forces them back into the violent relationship for want of resources to provide for themselves and often their children. The provision of housing is thus a primary need for the woman who wishes to end a violent relationship and it is likely too that financial assistance may be needed, at least for a while, until she manages to achieve economic independence by finding employment. For women with children, finding a job is perhaps especially difficult and they may require help in arranging suitable child care facilities.

The review of research has shown that at every stage there is a need for advice on the options open to a domestic violence victim, for accurate information on what type of help can be sought, from whom it can be obtained and how to set about obtaining it. Many people in society have only vague notions of what service agencies exist and, more particularly, of the nature of the services that are provided. Many domestic violence victims may not know of the civil law remedies that are available or how to obtain them. They may also not be aware of the existence of refuges or how to find them, or know of the duties imposed on local authorities by the *Housing Act, 1985*.

The problem of domestic violence has been shown to be not simply a problem of crime. Domestic violence manifests itself in diverse needs and brings with it a host of inter-related problems, problems which are outside the responsibilities of the criminal justice system. Their solution then requires the active involvement of other service agencies. Yet the research literature points to an unwillingness or, at least, a reluctance to accept such a responsibility. It almost seems as if each agency defines the problem in such a way that it is someone else's responsibility. Thus the police may perceive domestic violence as primarily a social, not criminal, problem. But social workers may perceive it as a criminal problem and, therefore, for the police to handle. The end result is that the victim can be left virtually helpless and may be passed from agency to agency.

However, although domestic violence is not *simply* a crime problem, it nevertheless remains such a problem. If the criminal justice system does not treat it as seriously as other crime problems, characterises it as primarily a private family matter, or adopts, as the Women's National Commission have described it, "an exaggerated respect for the closed doors of the family citadel", then the criminal justice system may signal to other agencies and to the wider public that domestic violence is a problem with which we should not be too concerned. This could result in relative indifference and inaction on all fronts. Although it seems unlikely that the response of the criminal justice system, *on its own*, will be sufficient to combat domestic violence or to deal with the diverse problems it brings in its wake, it is arguable that that response is nevertheless both necesary and potentially very important. The symbolic nature of law — its declaratory and denunciatory functions — is important in shaping climates of opinion. The criminal law is after all a normative statement. It sets the boundaries of acceptable behaviour. It is a statement of how people ought to behave and what will happen if they do not do so. But if the codes of behaviour set by the law are frequently broken and there is little enforcement of the law then the message conveyed may be that the behaviour proscribed by law is not really worth bothering about. The law's response is important in itself, since domestic violence is criminal assault, in its potential effects on the reaction of other agencies and in setting a more general climate of opinion in which domestic violence is seen for what it is: a crime.

An effective response to domestic violence involves more than medically treating injuries and ensuring that the law is enforced. Unfortunately, the research literature points to an ineffectiveness on the part of all agencies who might be expected to provide different types of assistance. That failure appears to stem partly from attitudes and beliefs about the 'proper' roles for men and women in relationships: the man is seen as the 'head of the family', the 'master in his own home', the 'breadwinner' and the woman is the 'wife and mother', subordinate to her partner. Research studies have shown that any perceived challenge to that authority can lead to a man using violence to reassert his control, to bring his partner 'back into line' or put her 'back in her place'. Perhaps not unexpectedly, research has also demonstrated that those activities and beliefs are also found in the professionals who encounter problems of domestic violence. If domestic violence is to be effectively tackled, it will be necessary to confront these attitudes. The difficulties inherent in any attempt to do so are considerable, given how deeply entrenched they appear to be. But effective responses to the problem need to be directed both at short-term solutions — dealing with the immediate needs of victims — and at long-term measures aimed at the prevention of domestic violence by tackling the conditions which give rise to it. The two-pronged attacks are closely related and inter-dependent. It seems unlikely that short-term immediate measures will be effective unless they are conceived of as a component, albeit an essential component, of longer-term preventive measures.

Improving responses

Civil law remedies

The remedies provided by the civil law cannot have any effect if their existence is not generally known and it appears that often they are not. Although police officers may inform victims of the civil law procedures when called to domestic incidents, given the low rate of reporting of domestic violence to the police, this may help only relatively few victims. Consideration, therefore, needs to be given as to how best to raise levels of knowledge and awareness and to inform victims of domestic violence of the remedies which are available and how they may be used.

Civil procedures have been criticised as being cumbersome, lengthy and subject to many delays. This is thought to add to victims' fears and open up the possibility of retaliatory violence. Delays can occur in a number of ways, for example, through the general judicial reluctance to grant *ex parte* injunctions. This is a difficult matter to resolve since to ensure a fair hearing the husband should be brought to court. It is sometimes suggested that there may be a case for greater use of *ex parte* injunctions if every effort has been made to serve notice and the husband is thought to be deliberately being evasive. Delays may also occur through the difficulty of locating available judges quickly enough, especially at weekends. One option for overcoming this difficulty might be the listing by courts of available judges and 'on call' rota systems to cover periods when courts do not usually sit.

The practice of restricting injunctions to a three month time limit has also been shown by research to aggravate victims' problems by not allowing sufficient time to make suitable arrangements, especially with regard to accommodation. Moreover, powers of arrest are attached only infrequently and yet, without such powers, the woman granted an injunction which her husband breaches has to apply to the court for her husband to be charged with contempt and has to serve notice on him that she has done so. The obstacles are therefore considerable. Injunctions without attached powers of arrest have been described as 'worthless'. Consideration needs to be given as to whether injuctions should *normally* carry a power of arrest and whether this should only be dispensed with where there is strong evidence that it is unnecessary. Moreover, the three month time limit applied to arrest powers has also been criticised as too restrictive. There may be a case for issuing new practice guidelines which raise the time limits. Breaches of injunction are sometimes dealt with only by way of a judicial reprimand. It might be questioned how far such reprimands will deter future additional breaches and whether other responses might be more successful in doing so.

There has been no systematic study at a national level of the operation of civil law procedures. Such research could be useful in establishing regional patterns, variations and good practice. The dissemination of such research might lead to greater consistency in practice.

Although the victim of domestic violence has civil law remedies available to her, the obstacles encountered in obtaining them are considerable. It demands courage and determination to put the procedures in motion, courage and determination at a time when most victims feel demoralised. One alternative might be to remove the responsibility for seeking the protection of the law from the individual woman to some other body. No doubt there would be some difficulty in involving the police further in matters of civil law, but such procedures have been developed elsewhere. In New South Wales in Australia, for example, legislation passed in 1983 to deal with domestic violence created, *inter alia*, a new procedure whereby in cases where there is a reasonable belief that domestic violence is likely to occur either victims or police officers can apply to the courts for an Apprehended Domestic Violence Order. The grounds for making such orders include molestation and harassment and the order itself carries restrictions on the spouse's conduct for a period of up to six months. This order does not replace the right of the victim to seek an injunction under the civil law; rather it adds to the total procedures available.

Criminal law

Some research studies have questioned whether domestic violence should be covered by the same laws as regulate violence between strangers. This is not a step towards de-criminalisation, but rather a suggestion that consideration could be given to creating a new offence specifically concerned with domestic violence — spouse assault, for example. The evidentiary problems involved in the prosecution of domestic violence under existing law have been discussed earlier. A new form of offence could take these into account. This is a matter which obviously needs consideration in some depth and might be best referred to the Criminal Law Revision Committee. It is an option which perhaps need not be dismissed too lightly since there may be valuable lessons to be learned from jurisdictions which deal with domestic violence as a distinct nominate crime (see Freeman, 1979).

The police response

It is no doubt true that many of the incidents described by the police as domestic 'disputes' or 'disturbances' involve behaviour which stops short of violence. It is also the case, however, that many do involve violence and regarding all as a single category of 'domestics' (which also includes landlord/tenant disputes and rows between neighbours) may serve to confuse the issue and, indeed, to detract from the violent nature of the assaults. There is a very real need to distinguish disputes stopping short of violence (whilst recognising that there may be a potential for violence to develop) from those where assaults have occurred. It might be questioned whether sending officers to an incident armed only with the information that it is a 'domestic' is adequate. Police forces could consider whether it would be beneficial to produce guidelines for those who take emergency telephone calls

91

and who dispatch officers to the scene in order to better enable them to distinguish the various types of dispute and to establish whether violence has occurred, has been threatened, or is likely to occur. A set of questions might be developed to ensure that adequate enquiries are made during the course of telephone calls to elicit sufficient information to determine appropriate action.

One of the issues which arose out of the research on police responses was the recording and information retrieval systems on domestic violence used by the police. The effectiveness of any organisation depends, in part, on the information which is available to it. A way forward here might be for domestic incidents to be recorded separately and note made of whether or not violence has taken place (or has been threatened) and the nature of any violence used. The incident record books and station message pads would need to be included in such a recording system so that as full a picture as possible could be gained. The research literature also pointed to the high level of 'no-criming' in relation to domestic violence. Forces may wish to examine their 'no-criming' procedures and to determine whether, in fact, their own practices — for example, allowing a 'cooling-off period', asking the victim in front of her assailant whether she wishes to press charges or repeatedly asking the victim if she *really* wants to proceed — encourage victims to withdraw allegations which are then 'no-crimed'. Although some allegations may be malicious — and there could be no argument against 'no-criming' in such cases — victims may not wish to proceed for a variety of reasons, not least of which is fear of further retaliatory violence. To automatically 'no-crime' those instances might be seen as inappropriate. In acknowledgement of victims' fears in relation to pursuing complaints, Home Office Circular 69/1986 called for a clear distinction to be drawn between unsubstantiated and false complaints regarding rape and serious sexual assault. It laid down that the only complaints which were to be 'no-crimed' were those where there was a complete retraction of the complaint *and* an admission of fabrication. Consideration could be given as to whether such advice to police forces should also extend to cases of domestic violence.

If use was made of such domestic violence information systems, local police could then be in a position of knowing the history or pattern of offending in any particular case rather than having to respond to every incident in a vacuum. Such information systems might better equip the police to identify 'high risk' families or to distinguish cases where crisis intervention techniques may have a chance of success from those where a legal response is required. The existence of injunctions would also need to be recorded in this system. Such systems ought to provide a more accurate assessment of the incidence of domestic violence which if they were brought to the attention of other local agencies could, in turn, aid the development of appropriate and co-ordinated services. Forces may wish to consider whether it would be appropriate to appoint Domestic Violence Liaison Officers, at say divisional level, whose responsibility would be to ensure the improved quality of police response and the development of links with other agencies.

The research literature also points to the difficulties experienced by individual officers when there are no clear force policy guidelines. Clear policies not only achieve greater consistency in individual cases but also, it has been argued in research from North America, help to promote more positive attitudes towards dealing with domestic violence. Some of the important issues identified in the research which would need to be addressed in the formulation of such a policy are those to do with arrest, the appropriate use of crisis intervention techniques and the circumstances in which to charge and pass the case to the Crown Prosecutor for decisions on prosecution.

One of the factors which has been brought out in the research is the tendency for the police to 'downgrade' violence in domestic incidents. Thus incidents where the injuries sustained could justify ABH or GBH charges may be downgraded to common assault and the victim advised to pursue a private prosecution. Arguably, if the evidence exists of severe violence, then it ought to be handled in that way. Moreover, placing the responsibility for prosecution on the individual victim may be inappropriate, given the nature and circumstances of the offence. This is a view now taken in many parts of the United States, Canada and Australia where, within recent years, the police have been charged with this responsibility.

Police arrest rates in domestic violence cases have been shown to be very low. There seems to be a presumption *against* arrest. Issues surrounding the argument for increased use of arrest are complex, particularly with regard to the deterrent function of arrest. Obviously, not every 'domestic dispute' warrants arrest but in formulating police force guidelines consideration needs to be given to whether in all domestic *violence* cases there should be a presumption *in favour* of arrest and whether failure to arrest should perhaps require an officer to provide written explanation of his/her actions. The available information, albeit restricted as it is, suggests that arrest can be an effective strategy, more effective than other traditional responses. Arrest not only underscores the seriousness of the incident and demonstrates to the victim that her right to police protection will not be denied, but it has also been found to be effective in deterring further repetition of violence. Whether or not arrest should be mandatory is another question. This is an approach which has been adopted, for example, in some American states. It, however, seems unrealistic and would run contrary to traditional police discretion which extends over many areas of the criminal law.

There is a tendency to see arrest and crisis intervention techniques as alternatives. That need not be the case. The London, Ontario, model successfully combines both. It is, indeed, arguable that they ought to be seen as complementary, and perhaps particularly where arrests have been made in incidents involving couples who are resolved to 'try again' rather than to separate. Moreover, the available evidence suggests that crisis intervention when used as the sole or main strategy is largely ineffective. It was suggested earlier in this review that it is a technique which is probably more suited to cases where disputes have not escalated into violence. It can also be questioned whether the police should play any part in counselling techniques. Their training does not equip them for such a role and there is a reluctance to become involved in 'social work'. Whilst all officers should possibly receive some training in general crisis management techniques and social skills so that domestic violence — and other sensitive incidents — are dealt with in an appropriate manner, the sort of intensive training necessary to make the police specialists would not seem the best use of resources. What might be considered a more appropriate responsibility for the police to shoulder is that they inform victims of where help of this type may be obtained and that they ensure that the appropriate referrals are made. Alternatively, consideration could be given to developing more formal liaison strategies on the lines of the London, Ontario, model. This would have the built-in advantage of shared information systems, less likelihood of communication failures and, potentially, the encouragement of better understanding between professionals.

What also comes out of the research is the importance of liaison with other bodies since domestic violence has such diverse aspects. At the very least, police officers need to know of the services that are available if they are to inform victims of where they might find help. Consideration could be given to the preparation of a brief pamphlet, booklet or even card which sets out basic information, including telephone numbers, on where help can be sought. (This is an approach which has been widely used in Canada.) This could be given to all victims when the police are called to domestic incidents irrespective of whether violence has actually occurred. If this option were adopted then it would be necessary to consider the language needs of ethnic minority victims. Another possibility might be the police providing agencies with details as to whom they have given such information, together with some indication as to whether or not the victim would welcome being contacted.

Training is of obvious importance. It is important for all agencies, however, for the research literature points to a basic lack in the way all professional agencies deal with domestic violence. A discussion of training might, therefore, best be left until after an examination of what improvements other agencies can make individually to their responses.

The prosecution process

The complex arguments which pertain to the issue of arrest are also applicable to the question of prosecution. On the one hand, prosecution can be seen as likely to aggravate conflict between the partners in a relationship, perhaps leading to an escalation in violence. On the other hand, it can be argued that no violence, whether between family members or strangers, should be tolerated and that it is the responsibility of the whole of the criminal justice system, not just the police, to ensure this. Moreover, it can also be argued that the very nature of domestic violence — its recurrent nature, increasing frequency of attacks and escalating severity of each assault — makes prosecution even more appropriate. Since prosecution is a comparatively rare event and research has tended to concentrate on police responses, to the relative neglect of other facets of the criminal justice system, the impact of prosecution on the prevention of further domestic assaults is unclear.

The Sherman and Berk (1984) study in Minneapolis appears to suggest that arrest alone, without subsequent charge and prosecution, can have a substantial impact in deterring further domestic assaults. However, the period in which this was assessed was limited to the six month follow-up of the study. The longer-term impact needs to be evaluated. It seems unlikely that without strengthening the impact of arrest in some way — whether or not that involves prosecution — that the effect of one arrest will be very strong or long-lasting in eliminating domestic violence, especially in those families in which it has been a common practice over many years. Moreover, the deterrent effect of arrest could become very short-lived if abusers discovered that this was all that would happen to them. Canadian research evidence (Dutton, 1986; 1987), limited though it is, lends support to this view. It is also questionable whether the police would continue to follow pro-arrest policies if other parts of the criminal justice system (prosecutors, magistrates and judges) failed to proceed in such cases or passed sentences or made disposals which were regarded as inappropriately lenient. There is a further problem with a system which relies on arrest alone and that involves civil liberties. It might well be thought that it would be a questionable practice for the police to be encouraged to routinely arrest and to hold suspects in custody without bringing charges.

A possible way forward might include the use in this country of more diversionary options and, where prosecution ensues, a greater range of sentencing options — as has become standard practice in many parts of North America. It has been stated earlier in this review that there is a need to distinguish domestic arguments which stop short of violence from those which might result in the relatively isolated use of slight physical force and from domestic conflict where violence is a recurrent, systematic, severe and deliberate act. Although the use of any violence is not to be condoned, some might argue that isolated incidents of a minor nature are perhaps almost likely to occur at some point in all or most close human relationships. Intervention at this point — through the use of counselling or therapy — might help to prevent such arguments from escalating into systematic brutality. Where the injury involved is slight and there is no evidence that it is one more incident in a sequence of assaults, it may be judged appropriate not to resort to prosecution but instead to use diversion. Consideration could be given as to whether formal cautioning might be appropriate for such cases. (Cautioning, however, is dependent upon the offender admitting he has committed an offence.) If this were done, the parties could be strongly advised to seek voluntary counselling.

Where violence results in more than slight injury and is part of a sequence of systematic assaults, then it could well be argued that prosecution is the more appropriate course of action. If treatment and counselling programmes were developed in this country as they have been in the United States and more recently, on an experimental basis, in Scotland they could form part of the range of available sanctions since fining or imprisoning an offender may only result in more direct hardship to the victim and the family where it is not intended to end the relationship. For example, a treatment programme could be made a condition of

95

a probation order. Currently, such a programme could not be used in conjunction with suspended sentences of imprisonment but again this is a matter which could be given further thought. It seems likely that assessment of the offender would need to be made before ordering participation in any particular type of programme. Given that research suggests that domestic violence occurs because offenders believe they can 'get away with it', careful monitoring of compliance seems to be called for and there may well be a case for failure being subjected to other sanctions of a more punitive nature to ensure that the message is clearly conveyed that the court 'means business'. The nature of some domestic violence is, however, so severe and prolonged that immediate imprisonment may be judged the only appropriate course of action.

Where the decision is taken to prosecute, then research has demonstrated that it is important that delays in bringing the matter to court are kept to a minimum. This helps minimise any risk of the victim wishing to withdraw — a risk which, however, has been noted as being, if not a myth, greatly exaggerated and most usually caused by legal delays and lack of support. Thus, it may be helpful, also, if victims receive emotional support during the period leading up to the court hearing — such developments in Canada could have lessons for this country. Women's Aid and the National Association of Victim Support Schemes could have an important role to play in this respect. Moreover, delays are thought to increase the probability of retaliatory violence and thus there is a need to ensure that the victim is protected during this period. Since most offenders will be released prior to the case coming to court, it might be thought advisable that some form of protection order is made part of the conditions of release. Finally, more attempt could be made to place less reliance on direct victim testimony and more on corroborating evidence as is happening in North America.

The medical profession and social services

Professional associations in medicine, nursing, health visiting and social services could increase their potential value in dealing with domestic violence by considering how best to respond appropriately to the problem. The lessons from Canada, for example, could be adopted here. Training programmes and codes of good practice could be developed; check lists could be drawn up to provide step-by-step guidelines for use in questioning suspected or known victims of domestic violence; encouragement could be given to liaison with and referral to other agencies; and data recording systems could be developed to help estimate the extent of the problem and to carefully record details of visits and injuries which might be used as evidence for cases that are prosecuted. All surgeries, casualty departments and offices of social services departments could display posters on domestic violence and other literature giving information on sources of help.

Another role that might be appropriate for social workers is that of a 'broker' between services. Advice could be given to individual women and appropriate referrals made to other agencies — to refuges, solicitors, housing departments and the police. Social workers could also ensure at a local level that there is provision of adequate and well co-ordinated services. It may, however, not be appropriate for social work departments to take on this role themselves, and certainly whoever did so would require the co-operation of other services and full commitment to the ideal of inter-agency co-operation. A different structure might have to be set up to develop this and to ensure that it was not dominated by the ideals of only one agency. But whatever structure was seen as being appropriate it seems inconceivable that social workers would not have a part to play in it. Until that development, a 'broker's role' in individual cases might well aid victims in their search for help.

The legal profession

Local law societies could do much to ensure that solicitors are provided with basic information on the services which are available for domestic violence victims so that they can advise clients accordingly. Some solicitors' firms may have little experience of such cases; others may be reluctant to take on such cases. Local law societies might wish to consider whether it would be appropriate to draw up lists of firms in their areas who have experience of such cases. This list could be circulated amongst all solicitors so that those who do not wish to accept domestic violence cases can advise potential clients of other firms offering some specialist experience in this area. Local law societies might also consider ensuring that agencies outside the profession which are relevant to domestic violence — the police, local doctors, social work departments, Citizens Advice Bureaux, local refuges — are also aware of particular firms which have developed expertise in such cases. Again, local law societies could arrange seminars or conferences on domestic violence which could serve to inform lawyers of the complex and diverse problems associated with domestic violence.

Training

The research evidence reviewed here points to the need for training courses for all agencies concerned with domestic violence — police, prosecutors, magistrates, judges, doctors, nurses, health visitors, social workers, lawyers. Indeed, given the complexity and inter-relatedness of the issues, there may well be a case for the consideration of interdisciplinary training. Locally based multi-disciplinary workshops might well help in this direction. Such initiatives could usefully complement training programmes run by individual organisations for their own members. It would seem important that all training should pull from the experience and knowledge of personnel outside the narrow confines of the specific discipline concerned. Involving refuge workers, for example, and, perhaps, victims themselves might be an appropriate strategy. Innovation and experimentation seem to be called for. Visits to refuges need not be ruled out as a means of familiarising professionals with problems experienced by victims. Domestic violence could be a topic covered in both the basic training of all professional and in-service refresher training courses.

Training could be broader than merely encompassing the scope of action of particular agencies. Insight should be given into the nature of domestic violence, its likely escalation into frequent and severe violence, the physical and psychological effects on victims and the consequences of inaction. The importance of a sympathetic approach and of listening and understanding problems from a victim's perspective could be taught to all agency personnel. Personnel could be sensitized to the problems associated with domestic violence. In particular, it might be argued that staff within one organisation should understand the role of those in other organisations and should be made knowledgeable about the provisions of legislation (including local authority housing legislation), the locations of refuges and victims' rights to social security benefits. The importance of liaison and inter-agency referral comes out of all the research reviewed here. The 'myths' or generally prevalent beliefs which serve to inhibit action (for example, that of 'victim reluctance') need to be challenged by reference to research findings. Attitudes and beliefs about the nature not only of domestic violence but also, more generally, about the nature of families, the role of men and women within them, and the privacy of the family unit have been shown to be crucial in shaping agencies' responses and need confronting in training. Given the importance of such attitudes and beliefs to agency action or inaction, any training programme which failed to tackle this, which failed to question 'taken for granted' assumptions and which failed to question whether a point is reached when efforts to keep families together have serious consequences might well be considered deficient.

Housing

The need to provide adequate housing both in the short and the long term has been discerned as a central component of any programme to tackle the problems associated with domestic violence. The role of local authorities is especially important in this area. As with so much of the information available on domestic violence, what is known about how local authorities interpret their duties under the *Housing Act 1985* tends to come from surveys of the experiences of women who are victims of domestic violence. Brailey's (1985) study of the policies and practices of four local authority housing departments in Scotland goes beyond this. She focussed not solely on women's experiences but also analysed local authority records, including committee minutes and policy reports, and interviewed senior officials. If there were more research of this type which not only monitored how local authorities carried out their legal duties but examined the attitudes which shape the policies which are formulated this would considerably expand our knowledge. This research, however, points to — and pleas have been made for — more flexibility in the kinds of approaches which are adopted; more flexibility in the type of housing stock provided, for example, to enable two or three women and their children to share a house, is required. The research which is available suggests the need for more sensitive housing policies and the need for more prompt action.

Refuges

The value of refuges both in terms of providing immediate emergency shelter and aiding the process of recovery through the mutual support given has been commented on in a large number of research studies. The Women's National Commission Report (1985), the Report of the United Nations Expert Group on Violence in the Family (1986) and the Final Communique of the Council of Europe Colloquy on Violence Within the Family (1987) also pay tribute to the refuge movement. Indeed, it is the one service with which victims express high levels of satisfaction, despite the often very inadequate standard of housing provided and the overcrowding which prevails. One of the main problems experienced by the refuge movement is both the inadequacy and the uncertainty of funding. This is complicated by the many agencies who have responsibility for various aspects of domestic violence. Pahl (1985) notes that the Convention of Scottish Local Authorities has recommended a tripartite responsibility involving central government and local authority housing and social work departments. A more novel approach, which need not be dismissed out of hand, is that adopted by some states in the United States where the cost of marriage licences has been raised to help fund refuges. Further consideration could also be given to the possibility of using money provided by the voluntary sector — by Rotary, for example, as happens in Canada.

Inter-agency co-operation

The suggestion that there should be co-operation between agencies is not new. It has been explicitly acknowledged throughout this review in the stress which has been placed on the need for advice to be available on the sources of potential assistance, on the importance of referrals, on the recognition that domestic violence entails a host of related problems requiring the active involvement of a diverse range of services, and on the need for training programmes for individual agencies to ensure that the services of other agencies are adequately covered in training. A multi-agency approach is consciously being adopted as a matter of policy in other countries (L'orange, 1986; Pence, 1983; 1985; Walker, 1985; Wood, 1986). It has also been recommended by the United Nations Expert Group on Violence in the Family (1986), the Council of Europe Colloquy on Violence Within the Family (1987) and, in this country, by the Women's National Commission (1985). A Home Office circular (69/1986) to all Chief Officers of Police recommended that consideration be given to whether or not the development of such an approach would be appropriate in local areas. Some police forces, for example the West Midlands, were already participating in multi-agency working groups on domestic violence at the time the Women's National Commission working group was receiving evidence, and others may have followed suit as Tottenham in the Metropolitan Police District has done in response to the new force orders.

It seems likely that it is only through the development of such an approach that a really integrated and co-ordinated approach at all levels will evolve which will help victims and which will aid the process of not solely responding to a problem but also moving towards its prevention. The government of New South Wales, for example, has established a Domestic Violence Committee to operate at state level. This committee comprises representatives of the State Departments of Police, Health, Youth and Community Services, Housing, Education, Attorney General and Justice in addition to community representatives. Any matter concerning domestic violence which arises in the respective departments' responsibilities is referred to the Committee which is charged with monitoring the implementation of the domestic violence legislation reforms enacted within the last few years and with seeking to further the development of the multi-faceted domestic violence programme which has been established. In Canada this approach has been adopted at both Federal and provincial level (for example, in Ontario). Consideration could be given as to whether this type of approach would be beneficial here. If so, the Inter-Ministerial Group on Women's Issues which is chaired by a Home Office Minister might be an appropriate forum.

Although national bodies may be important, there is perhaps a greater need to ensure that a multi-agency approach is effected at local level and that co-operation and co-ordination within specific localities is tailored to the particular problems of that locality. There is no clear argument favouring one agency as opposed to another as the instigator of such an approach: it may differ from one area to the next. The important point is that someone takes the lead — becomes the broker — in bringing together representatives from the various agencies — the police, social services, housing, the law, medicine, Women's Aid, Citizens Advice Bureaux, Victim Support Schemes and self-help groups such as Gingerbread. The group could function to ensure that organisations within it were fully aware of the services provided by others and from whom help might be sought. For this purpose, 'fact packs' could be produced on the work of all the agencies for use by individual members of each.[1]

Such groups might do much to improve local knowledge and to publicise the problem of domestic violence and the sources of help available within the locality. They could regularly review the provisions which are made and seek ways of improving them, for example, by considering the establishment of a family consultancy service on the lines of the London, Ontario, model.

Consideration could also be given as to whether such a team could go beyond this role and could become involved in the management of individual cases. It has already occurred in the multi-agency working group in which the West Midlands police participate (Women's National Commission, 1985), though it is perhaps a more difficult role to achieve. Different agencies have different philosophies on which they operate and different definitions of the essential nature of problems and how they are best tackled. There would have to be a concerted attempt to ensure that any local structure which was developed was not dominated by the ideals of any one agency. But participation within such a group could lead to better understanding between different agencies and the gradual development of a shared outlook as to how best to respond to domestic violence. There are, however, other problems in achieving such co-operation, not least, that of confidentiality in

---

[1] The Home Office is currently funding a developmental research project to produce such a fact pack. Agencies' perceptions of its usefulness will be evaluated.

sharing information about incidents of domestic violence which have occurred within families, about incidents where domestic violence is suspected but not definitely known, and about families who are thought to be at risk of domestic violence. For example, people seeking help from doctors or lawyers often do so in the knowledge of the confidentiality of the doctor/patient and solicitor/client relationship. Issues of confidentiality would need to be carefully considered, perhaps drawing on experience of dealing with other family problems such as child abuse.

The need for community awareness

However much agencies, either individually or together, work towards improving the services they provide, it can be argued that their response can only be enhanced by increased social and community awareness of the problem. Community education and publicity programmes would help in this direction. In addition to providing advice to victims on where they might seek help, such programmes could help to create a more general awareness among the public of the reality of the problem of domestic violence and to provide a clear message that it is a crime which must be taken seriously. Again this has been recommended by the United Nations and the Council of Europe and has been put into practice in Canada.

A variety of means could be used. Posters, for example, could be placed on all forms of public transport; retailers encouraged to display them in shops; local health authorities could ensure that they were displayed in hospitals and doctors' surgeries; and local government authorities could display them in social work and housing departments and in libraries. Central government could consider including publicity leaflets in letters about child benefit allowances in the same way that TV licence reminders have been used to convey messages about licence evasion and car tax reminders have been used to convey messages on the prevention of autocrime. The media have a part to play here. Local radio and television could be particularly influential in mounting a public education campaign. Crisis telephone lines might be a useful accompaniment to any such intensive campaign so that specific advice could be given on the services available within any one area.

The needs of ethnic minority communities would have to be considered. Little is known in this country of the domestic violence occurring within such groups: it is an issue which would benefit from further exploration. The pamphlets and information leaflets used in any educational publicity campaigns would need to be available in the principal languages of the ethnic minority groups living in Britain. If crisis telephone lines were established, there might also be a need for multilingual interpreters. The role of religious and community leaders within such communities could be particularly important. Authoritative statements from respected influential members denouncing domestic violence and advising that outside help be sought may encourage victims to break their silence.

Underlying issues

So far attention has been concentrated upon how victims' needs can best be met in the short term. Emphasis has, therefore, been placed on how *responses* to domestic violence might be improved. But few disagree with the old adage that 'prevention is better than cure'. The question to be addressed is how prevention can best be achieved? The ultimate goal must be to move towards a society in which domestic violence is not tolerated: a society in which social, cultural, legal and economic factors are such as to inhibit its development and which responds swiftly when it does appear. This calls for far-reaching changes. Although some domestic assaults may result from the actions of psychopaths, alcoholics and depressives, the extent of the problem — the fact that it is not a rare and isolated occurrence — is such as to suggest that such an explanation for all domestic violence has to be rejected. Instead, there is increasing recognition in the research literature and, indeed, by the international conferences which have been mentioned in this review that any policies designed to prevent domestic violence have to look to the norms, attitudes, beliefs and the structural conditions which both give rise to and support it.

This involves confronting how as a society we construct and define behaviour termed 'masculine' and 'feminine'; how we ascribe roles within marriage; and how those processes regulate the position of women. These have important implications for how as a society we socialise children. The educational system has a potentially important part to play in the furtherance of long-term prevention. Not only is it important that gender stereotypes are questioned, but it is also important that the message is conveyed that violence is not a legitimate response to problems. In Ontario, Canada, this has been taken on board in the development of schools' curricula. The economic dependency of many women has also been identified in the research literature as contributing to domestic violence, especially since it makes leaving violent relationships difficult and may also force women who have left their homes to return. This would suggest that greater attempts have to be made to enhance the economic independence of women. Attempts to eliminate explicit discrimination against women in the field of employment have been made in recent years and progress has been achieved, but there is a continuing need to try to augment that progress and to expose and tackle more implicit forms of discrimination.

None of this is likely to be achieved easily or quickly. Arguably, however, it is through the promotion of greater equality between men and women — and the promotion of greater respect for that equality — coupled with concentrated efforts to ensure that children are not taught — do not learn — to regard violence as an acceptable form of problem solution that real progress in the prevention of domestic violence will be made. The evidence from the United States is encouraging in this respect. Straus and Gelles (1986) attribute much of the observed decrease in domestic violence between 1975 and 1985 to:

> "...a combination of changed attitudes and norms...changes in the family, in the economy, in the social acceptability of family violence, in alternatives available for women, in social control processes, and in the availability of treatment and prevention services."

Such changes may not eliminate all domestic violence but may do much to reduce it to the level of a comparatively rare event.

Further research

Much of the information on domestic violence which has been covered in this review has been gained from studies of women who have been victims and often from victims who have sought shelter in refuges. Such studies often have to rely on relatively small sample sizes. There is clearly a need to move away from reliance on this type of research. At the present time, no comprehensive national survey using representative samples of the general population has been undertaken in this country. Yet the kind of information produced by such a survey it could be argued would be beneficial. Theoretically, for example, it should allow comparisons to be made between those who have experience of domestic violence (either as victims or, less likely, as abusers) with those who have not. Such a survey ought to provide more accurate estimates of the extent of the problem than those currently available and ought to be able to shed light on the factors giving rise to the problem. This information would be of value in developing policies to tackle it. Moreover, if a national survey were backed by a series of locally based surveys that, too, would aid local decision-making and policy planning. However, it seems most unlikely that reliable quantitative estimates of the extent of domestic violence will ever be achieved. It is not a problem which lends itself easily to the methods of survey research: for a variety of reasons, there is a reluctance to admit to being a victim of this type of crime and it is probable that there would be greater reluctance to admit to being an abuser. Given the substantial financial costs involved in national surveys, this may not then represent the best use of resources. It might be worth exploring whether locally based surveys, which cost less, would yield the level of information desired. If this were done then they should be carried out in localities which would yield information, since there is a distinct lack of detailed knowledge at present, about the extent and nature of domestic violence occurring within ethnic minority groups on these matters. Indeed the whole question of domestic violence and ethnic minorities needs further exploration. It is not just information on its extent and nature which is lacking. Little is known, for example, on whether there is differential reporting to the police and other agencies and how, if help is sought, those agencies respond to the problem in ethnic minority communities and what satisfaction is expressed by victims about any help that is given. There are now a number of refuges which cater exclusively for women from ethnic minorities and yet there is still a lack of basic information.

There is also a case for encouraging more research of the type conducted by Dobash and Dobash (1979) which they have termed 'context specific' — that is, concentrating on delineating the specific characteristics, mechanisms and conditions that give rise to domestic violence as a particular form of behaviour. Here it is important that attempts are made to obtain comparison groups of couples in whose relationship domestic violence has not featured. This might aid our understanding of domestic violence by revealing important characteristics or conditions which have previously been overlooked.

The criminal justice system

Research which focuses upon the various agents of the criminal justice system should make attempts to compare their responses to domestic violence with responses to other forms of non-domestic violence. Moreover, research should attempt to test Sanders' (1987) hypothesis that the important distinguishing factor is not whether violence occurs in the domestic setting or between strangers, but whether there is an element of public disorder involved. This applies to police and prosecution decision-making and to sentencing practice.

The police

There is conflicting evidence about the extent to which women withdraw complaints of domestic violence. It is a matter which, therefore, requires further investigation. The reasons for withdrawal need to be examined more closely: in particular, the question of how far the police, by their practices, contribute to those withdrawals should be addressed. On a related issue, closer attention needs to be paid to 'no-criming' practices.

Much of the research describing police attitudes to domestic violence has relied upon victims' accounts which have been used to infer police attitudes. More information needs to be gathered directly from interviews with serving officers (as in the studies by Edwards (1986b and d) and the PSI team (1987)). This would allow for comparisons to be made between male and female officers, different ranks and different age groups. It could explore what measures police officers think would better enable them to deal with domestic violence; for example, the development of specialist police teams to provide counselling after initial intervention; working with trained social workers; and developing inter-agency co-operation.

It is also important that research on the police goes beyond analysis of records and interviews with officers. Direct observational studies of how police actually deal with domestic violence incidents are an important source of information. Actual behaviour can then be contrasted with expressed attitudes. Observation can distinguish different styles of response and of manner, different kinds of actions taken, and different kinds of advice given on referrals which might have implications for outcome, for victims' satisfaction and for police training. Observation can assess whether or not officers who have received training on domestic violence put that training into practice and how their responses compare with officers who have not been so trained.

The Police and Criminal Evidence Act 1984 gave new powers of arrest to the police in dealing with domestic violence. Research should, therefore, examine whether and how often those powers have been used and under what circumstances. One of the most important questions is whether arrest should be the normal policy in cases of domestic violence since it appears to prevent reoffending, as demonstrated by the Minneapolis experiment (Sherman and Berk, 1984). There is an argument in favour of replicating that experiment here though there could be ethical objections to its randomised nature. Moreover, the design of such a study would need to overcome the methodological difficulties discussed (supra pp.60-61) in relation to Sherman and Berk's experiment. If it is considered desirable to replicate the experiment, it should really go further and test the view that arrest, without subsequent prosecution, is a sufficient deterrent in itself. But if there are ethical objections to randomised arrest, then such objections would apply even more strongly to randomised prosecution. Whatever the final design — arrest or arrest and prosecution — there should be a longer follow-up period than the six months used in the Minneapolis experiment.

The prosecution process

The responses of agents involved at later stages in the criminal justice process require examination since little research has been conducted on these stages. The work of Wasoff (1982) and Sanders (1987) is instructive, though their evidence is at times conflicting and needs to be replicated using larger samples. A variety of research techniques — analysis of records, interviews with personnel and observation — are again needed to more fully understand the factors which influence their decision-making. In particular, the impact on levels of prosecution of the Crown Prosecution Service needs to be investigated. An examination of those cases which the police pass to the CPS with those which they do not appears appropriate. The relative influence of the general rule that there should be a realistic prospect of conviction and of more general attitudes towards domestic violence *per se* on prosecutors' decision-making needs to be studied. What are their attitudes towards using the powers given under PACE to compel spouses to give evidence? An examination of how often they are being used and with what results should be made. Again there is a need for long-term evaluation of both the impact of prosecution and of whether different types of sentence are more effective than others in deterring re-offending.

Counselling, mediation and treatment programmes

It was suggested in the body of the review that consideration should be given to evaluating, on an experimental basis, appropriate counselling, mediation and treatment programmes. Evidence from the United States on the use of mediation techniques is pessimistic but if they are established here it would be important to ensure that they were properly evaluated as to their effectiveness in preventing the re-occurrence of domestic violence. Questions to be examined would include whether one form was more successful than another and whether different types of intervention were appropriate to different types of offender. Similar types of consideration would have to be encompassed in evaluations of treatment programmes. Evaluation should also be made as to effectiveness of different methods of referral to the programme: self or agency referral; as a form of diversion from formal prosecution; and as a sentence of the court. Evaluation would need to be carried out over time and the criterion of success should be that the violence stops.

Agencies outwith the criminal justice system

The response of agencies outwith the criminal justice system have been shown to be important. Further research is needed here. It is perhaps particularly important that more studies are conducted into the operation of agencies themselves, how their policies are formulated and what considerations inform the shaping of those policies. The information gained from victims' accounts could usefully be

105

augmented through interviews with personnel and analyses of records. In the very important area of the provision of housing, local authorities' compliance with the *Housing Act, 1985* should be monitored.

Inter-agency co-operation

Multi-agency working groups such as those in which the West Midlands police and the Tottenham station in the Metropolitan Police District participate ought to be examined to see if lessons on 'best practice' can be gained for other areas who might be considering adopting such an approach.

Civil law remedies: their application

More needs to be known about how the remedies available under the civil law are being used. Research could also reveal the extent of regional variation commented on in a number of research studies. There is conflicting research evidence on whether solicitors prefer the magistrates' courts or the county courts for domestic violence cases. This is a question which requires further investigation. Such a study should encompass a comparison of the evidence accepted in different types of court, the factors considered important to both the granting of injunctions and to the attachment of powers of arrest and the speed with which cases are dealt in order to empirically test whether there is some basis for the views which have been advanced as to why one venue as opposed to the other is the preferred choice.

Need for longitudinal studies

The possible strategies which have been suggested for dealing with domestic violence should be seen as tentative. We have no way of knowing at present whether one approach would be better than another. There is thus a need for innovation and experimentation subject to evaluation before policies can be set with any degree of certainty that they will be effective. Most research has been retrospective, relying on individuals' memory for information. It is now time to set up a prospective longitudinal study to test the effects of different strategies.

Need for research on men

It has been said many times in this review that the knowledge gained about domestic violence rests to a very large extent on information which has been collected from women. By and large that is also true of the information we have on men who are abusers. A way needs to be found which would allow men to be subject to the same kind of detailed scrutiny. The problem, of course, is how to find a group of such co-operative male abusers. If formal modes of mediation and treatment programmes are established this might help solve the problem. Meanwhile, more attempts need to be made to interview men who are arrested and/or prosecuted though it is recognised that they may not be 'typical' of all abusers. Research could be carried out on the attitudes and backgrounds of such men and on the details of the violent incidents in which they have been involved in order that a better understanding of the causes as they perceive them can be gained. Questions requiring investigation include whether or nor there are different types of abusers and whether or not they are motivated by different types of factors, triggered by different stimuli. Such enquiries need not necessarily lead to an exclusive focus on individual or pathological factors. These factors could be important in determining whether it is necessary to develop different types of responses to deal with different types of abusers. Such research could also tackle questions on how the male world — workmates, friends, clubs etc — responds to domestic violence both in the specific case and in the abstract and how normative support for domestic violence is generated and sustained. Such research could lead to a fuller understanding of the phenomenon of domestic violence in order to aid efforts to reduce it.

References

Andrews, B. (1987). *Violence in Normal Families*. Paper presented at the Marriage Research Centre Conference on Family Violence, London, April 1987.

Babin, M. (1985). 'Crisis Intervention'. *RCMP Gazette*. 47, 2, 1-20.

Bae, R. P. (1981). 'Ineffective crisis intervention techniques: the use of the police'. *Journal of Crime and Justice*, 4, 61-82.

Banton, M. (1964). *The Policeman in the Community*. London: Tavistock Publications.

Bard, M. (1970). *Training Police as Specialists in Family Crisis Intervention*. Washington D.C.: Government Printing Office.

Bard, M. (1973). *Family Crises Intervention from Concept to Implementation*. Washington D.C.: US Government Printing Office.

Bard, M. and Zacker, J. (1971). 'The prevention of family violence: dilemmas of community intervention'. *Journal of Marriage and the Family,* 33, 4, 677-682.

Bard, M. and Zacker, J. (1974). 'Assaultiveness and alcohol use in family disputes: police perceptions'. *Criminology*. 12, 3, 281-292.

Baur, C. and Ritt, (1983). 'A husband is a beating animal'. *International Journal of Women's Studies*, 6, 2, 99-118.

Bedfordshire Police (1976). *Report on Acts of Domestic Violence Committed in the County between 1st February and 31st July 1976*.

Bell, D. J. (1984a). 'The police response to domestic violence'. *Police Studies,* 7, 1, 23-30.

Bell, D. J. (1984b). 'The police response to domestic violence: a replication study'. *Police Studies*, 7, 3, 136-144.

Bell, D. J. (1985). 'A multi-year study of Ohio urban, suburban and rural dispositions of domestic disputes'. *Victimology*, 10, 1-4, 301-310.

Berk, S. H. and Loseke, D. R. (1980). 'Handling family violence: situational determinants of police arrest in domestic disturbances'. *Law and Society Review*, 15, 2, 317-346.

Berk, R. A., Loseke, D. R., Berk, S. F. and Rauma, D. (1980). 'Bringing the cops back in: a study of efforts to make the criminal justice system more responsive to incidents of domestic violence'. *Social Science Research,* 9, 193-215.

Berk, R. A. and Newton, P. J. (1985). 'Does arrest really deter wife battery? An effort to replicate the findings of the Minneapolis Spouse Abuse Experiment'. *American Sociological Review*, 50, 2, 253-262.

Berk, R. A. and Sherman, L. W. (1985). 'Data collection strategies in the Minneapolis Domestic Assault Experiment'. In: Burstein, L., Freeman, H. E. and Rossi, P. H. (Eds.). *Collecting Evaluation Data*. Beverly Hills, California: Sage.

Binney, V., Harkell, G. and Nixon, J. (1981). *Leaving Violent Men: A Study of Refuges and Housing for Battered Women.* London: Women's Aid Federation, England.

Binney, V., Harkell, G. and Nixon, J. (1985). 'Refuges and housing for battered women'. In: Pahl, J. (ed.) *Private Violence and Public Policy.* London: Routledge and Kegan Paul.

Bittner, E. (1974). 'Florence Nightingale in pursuit of Willy Sutton: a theory of the police'. In: Jacob, H. (Ed.). *The Potential for Reform of Criminal Justice.* Beverly Hills, California: Sage.

Black, D. (1971). 'The social organisation of arrest'. *Stamford Law Review,* 23 (June) 1087-1111.

Black, D. (1980). *The Manners and Customs of the Police.* New York: Academic Press.

Blackstone, W. (1966). *Commentaries on the Laws of England.* (First published 1765) London: Dawsons.

Borkowski, M., Murch, M. and Walker, V. (1983). *Marital Violence. The Community Response.* London: Tavistock Publications.

Bowker, L. (1982). 'Police services to battered women: bad or not so bad?' *Criminal Justice and Behaviour,* 9, 4, 476-494.

Bowker, L. (1983). *Beating Wife Beating.* Lexington, Mass.: Lexington Books.

Brailey, M. (1985). 'Making the break'. In: Johnson, N. (Ed.). *Marital Violence.* Sociological Review Monograph. London: Routledge and Kegan Paul.

Brown, S. E. (1984). 'Police responses to wife beating: neglect of a crime of violence'. *Journal of Criminal Justice.* 12, 277-288.

Browning, J. (1984). *Stopping the Violence: Canadian Programmes for Assaultive Men.* Ottawa: National Clearinghouse on Family Violence, Ministry of Health and Welfare.

Buchanan, D. R. and Chasnoff, P. (1986). 'Family crisis intervention programmes: what works and what doesn't'. *Journal of Police Science and Administration.* 14, 2, 161-168.

Burris, C. A. and Jaffe, P. (1983). 'Wife abuse as a crime: the impact of police laying charges'. *Canadian Journal of Criminology*, 25, 3, 309-328.

Burris, C. A. and Jaffe, P. (1984). 'Wife battering: a well-kept secret'. *Canadian Journal of Criminology*. 26, 171-177.

Campbell, J. C. (1985). 'Beating of wives: a cross-cultural perspective'. *Victimology,* 10, 174-185.

Cannings, D. M. (1984). 'Myths and stereotypes—obstacles to effective police intervention in domestic disputes involving a battered women'. *Police Journal,* January, 43-55.

Carlson, B. E. (1977). 'Battered women and their assailants'. *Social Work.* 22, 455-460.

Chambers, G. and Millar, A. (1983). *Investigating Sexual Assault.* Edinburgh: HMSO (A Scottish Office Social Research Study).

Chapman, J. R. and Gates, M. (Eds.). (1978). *The Victimization of Women.* Beverly Hills, California: Sage.

Chatterton, M. (1983). 'Police work and assault charges'. In: Punch, M. (Ed.). *Control in the Police Organisation.* Cambridge, Mass: MIT Press.

Chester, R. and Streather, J. (1972). 'Cruelty in English divorce: some empirical findings'. *Journal of Marriage and the Family* 34, 4, 706-711.

Clifton, J. (1985). 'Refuges and self help'. In: Johnson, N. (Ed.). *Marital Violence.* Sociological Review Monograph 31. London: Routledge and Kegan Paul.

Cobbe, F. P. (1878). 'Wife torture in England'. *Contemporary Review.* April, 55-87.

Cohn, E. G. and Sherman, L. W. (1987). *Police Policy on Domestic Violence 1986: a national survey.* Paper presented to American Society of Criminology Meeting, Montreal, November 1987.

Coleman, C. A. and Bottomley, A. K. (1976). 'Police conceptions of crime and "no crime"'. *Criminal Law Review.* 5, 2, 344-360.

Colledge, M. and Bartholomew, R. (1980). 'The long-term unemployed: some new evidence'. *Employment Gazette,* January.

Couch, S. R. (1983). 'Research on wife abuse: a scan of the literature'. In: Costa, J. J. *Abuse of Women: legislation, reporting and prevention.* Lexington, Mass.: Lexington Books.

Crites, L. (1987). 'Wife abuse: the judicial record'. In: Crites, L. and Hepperle, W. (Eds). *Women, the Courts and Equality.* Beverly Hills: Sage.

Cumming, E., Cumming, I. and Edell, L. (1965). 'Policeman as philosopher, guide and friend'. *Social Problems.* 12 (Winter), 276-286.

Currie, D. (1985). 'Group model for men who assault their partners'. In: Sinclair, D. *Understanding Wife Assault. A Training Manual for Counsellors and Advocates.* Toronto: Ontario Government Bookstore.

Davies, P. W. (1982). 'Structured rationales for non-arrest: police stereotypes of domestic disturbance'. *Criminal Justice Review.* 6, 2, 8-15.

Deschner, J. (1984). *The Hitting Habit: anger control for battering couples.* New York: Free Press.

Dobash, R. E. and Dobash, R. P. (1979). *Violence Against Wives.* New York: The Free Press.

Dobash, R. E. and Dobash, R. P. (1981). 'Community response to violence against wives: charivari, abstract justice and patriarchy'. *Social Problems,* 28, 5, 563-581.

Dobash, R. E. and Dobash, R. P. (1984). 'The nature and antecedents of violent events'. *British Journal of Criminology,* 24, 3, 269-288.

Dobash, R. E., Dobash, R. P. and Cavanagh, K. (1985). 'The contact between battered women and social and medical agencies'. In: Pahl, J. (Ed.). *Private Violence and Public Policy.* London: Routledge and Kegan Paul.

Dolon, R., Hendricks, J. and Meagher, M. S. (1986). 'Police practices and attitudes towards domestic violence'. *Journal of Police Science and Administration,* 14, 3, 187-192.

Durbin, K. (1974). 'Wife beating'. *Ladies Journal,* (June). *Quoted in:* Martin, D. 'Battered women: society's problem'. In: Chapman, J. R. and Gates, M. (1978). *The Victimization of Women.* Beverly Hills, California: Sage.

Dutton, D. G. (1977). 'Domestic dispute intervention by police'. *Family Violence. Proceedings of a Symposium on Family Violence, March 1977, Vancouver.*

Dutton, D. G. (1984). *The Criminal Justice System Response to Wife Assault.* Ottawa: Ministry of the Solicitor General.

Dutton, D. G. (1986). 'The outcome of court mandated treatment for wife assault: a quasi-experimental evaluation'. *Violence and Victims* 1, 3, 163-175.

Dutton, D. G. (1987). *The Prediction of Recidivism in a Population of Wife Assaulters.* Paper presented at American Society of Criminology Meeting, Montreal, November 1987.

Edelson, J. L. and Gruzinski, R. J. (Forthcoming). *Treating Men who Batter: four years of outcome data from the domestic abuse project.*

Edwards, S. S. M. (1985a). 'Compelling a reluctant spouse: protection and the prosecution process'. *New Law Journal.* November, 1076-1078.

Edwards, S. S. M. (1985b). 'A socio-legal evaluation of gender ideologies in domestic violence, assault and spousal homicides'. *Victimology,* 10, pp 186-205.

Edwards, S. S. M. (1986a). 'The real risks of violence behind closed doors'. *New Law Journal* 136/628, 1191-1193.

Edwards, S. S. M. (1986b). *The Police Response to Domestic Violence in London.* London: Central London Polytechnic.

Edwards, S. S. M. (1986c). *Sex Role and Family Ideologies in Policing Domestic Violence: the London Study.* Paper presented to the World Congress on Victimology, Orlando, Florida, 9-13 July 1986.

Edwards, S. S. M. (1986d) 'Police attitudes and dispositions in domestic disputes: the London Study'. *Police Journal.* July, 230-241.

Ellis, D. (1987). *Policing Wife-Abuse: The Contribution Made by Domestic Disturbances to Deaths and Injuries Among Police Officers.* Paper presented at American Society of Criminology Meeting, Montreal, November 1987.

Elston, E., Fuller, J. and Murch, M. (1976). *Battered Wives. The Problems of Violence in Marriages as experienced by a Group of Petitioners in Undefended Divorce Cases.* Department of Social Work, University of Bristol.

Evason, E. (1982). *Hidden Violence.* Belfast: Farset Press.

Fagan, J. A., Steward, D. K. and Hansen, K. V. (1983). 'Violent men or violent husbands?: background factors and situational correlates'. In. Finkelhor, D. *et al.* (Eds.) *The Dark Side of Families.* Beverly Hills, California: Sage.

Faragher, T. (1985). 'The police response to violence against women in the home'. In: Pahl. J. (Ed.). *Private Violence and Public Policy.* London: Routledge and Kegan Paul.

Farrington, K. M. (1980). 'Stress and family violence'. In: Straus, M. A. Hotaling, G. T. (Eds.). *The Social Causes of Husband-Wife Violence.* Minneapolis, Minnesota: University of Minnesota Press.

Faulk, M. (1974). 'Men who assault their wives'. *Medicine, Science and the Law,* 14, 180-183.

FBI Uniform Crime Reports. (1978). *Crime in the United States.* Washington D.C.: U.S. Department of Justice.

Ferraro, K. J. and Johnson, J. M. (1982) 'How women experience battering: the process of victimization'. *Social Problems,* 30, 3, 325-339.

Fine, M. (1981). 'An injustice by any other name'. *Victimology,* 6, 48-58.

Flynn, J. P. (1977). 'Recent findings relating to wife abuse'. *Social Casework,* 58, 13-20.

Freeman, M. D. A. (1977). 'Le vice anglais? Wife battering in English and American law'. *Family Law Quarterly,* Fall, 199-251.

Freeman, M. D. A. (1979). *Violence in the Home.* Farnborough: Saxon House.

Freeman, M. D. A. (1980). 'Violence against women: does the legal system provide solutions or itself constitute the problem?' *British Journal of Law and Society,* 7, 2, 215-241.

Freeman, M. D. A. (1984). 'Legal ideologies, patriarchal precedents and domestic violence'. In: Freeman, M. D. A. (Ed.). *The State, the Law and the Family.* London: Tavistock Publications.

Freeman, M. D. A. (1985a). 'Doing his best to sustain the sanctity of marriage'. In: Johnson, N. (Ed.). *Marital Violence.* Sociological Review Monograph 31. London: Routledge and Kegan Paul.

Freeman, M. D. A. (1985b). "Towards a critical theory of family law". *Current Legal Problems.* 38, 153-185.

Freeman, M. D. A. (1987). *Dealing with Domestic Violence.* Bicester: CCH Editions Ltd.

Frieze, I. H. (1983). 'Investigating the causes and consequences of marital rape'. *Signs,* 8, 3, 532-553.

Garner, J. and Clemmer, E. (1986). *Danger to Police—Domestic Disturbances—A New Look.* Washington D.C.: National Institute of Justice.

Gayford, J. J. (1975) 'Wife battering: a preliminary survey of 100 cases'. *British Medical Journal,* (January), 194-197.

Gayford, J. J. (1976). 'Ten types of battered wives'. *Welfare Officer,* 25, 1, 5-9.

Gayford, J. J. (1978). 'Battered wives'. In: Martin, J. P. *Violence and the Family.* Chichester: John Wiley.

Gelles, R. J. (1974). *The Violent Home.* Beverly Hills, California: Sage.

Gelles, R. J. (1976). 'Abused Wives: why do they stay?' *Journal of Marriage and the family,* November, 659-669.

Gelles, R. J. (1977). 'No place to go: the social dynamics of marital violence'. In: Roy, M. (Ed.). *Battered Women.* New York: Van Nostrand Reinhold.

Gelles, R. J. (1983). 'An exchange/social control theory'. In: Finkelhor, D. *et al.* (Eds.). *The Dark Side of Families.* Beverly Hills, California: Sage.

Gelles, R. J. and Cornell, C. (1985). *Intimate Violence in Families.* Beverly Hills, California: Sage.

Gibson, E. (1975). *Homicide in England and Wales 1967-1971.* Home Office Research Study No. 31. London: HMSO.

Gibson, E and Klein, S. (1961). *Murder.* Studies in the Causes of Delinquency and Treatment of Offenders No. 4. London: HMSO.

Gibson, E. and Klein, S. (1969). *Murder 1957-1968.* Home Office Research Study No. 3. London: HMSO.

Gondolf, E. W. (1984). *Men Who Batter: How to Stop Their Abuse.* Paper presented at the Second National Conference for Family Violence Researchers, University of New Hampshire, August.

Gondolf, E. W. (1985a). 'Anger and oppression in men who batter: empiricist and feminist perspectives and their implications for research'. *Victimology,* 10, 311-324.

Gondolf, E. W. (1985b). *Men Who Batter: An Integrated Approach to Stopping Wife Abuse.* Holmes Beach Fl.: Learning Publications Inc.

Goolkasian, G. A. (1986). *Confronting Domestic Violence: the role of criminal court judges.* Washington D.C.: National Institute of Justice.

Greenblat, C. J. (1985). '"Don't beat your wife...unless". Premliminary findings on normative support for use of physical force by husbands' *Victimology,* 10, 221-241.

Grim, N. (1983). 'Domestic relations: legal responses to wife beating: theory and practice in Ohio'. *Akron Law Review,* 16, 4, 705-745.

Hamilton, R. (1984). 'Has the House of Lords abolished the Domestic Violence Act for Married Women'; *Legal Action,* March, 25-27.

Hanmer, J. and Saunders, S. (1983). 'Blowing the cover of the protective male. A community study of violence to women'. In: Gamarnakow, E. *et al.* (Eds.) *The Public and the Private: social patterns of gender relations.* London: Heinemann.

Hanmer, J. and Saunders, S. (1984). *Well-Founded Fear.* London: Hutchinson and Co.

Hanmer, J. and Stanko, E. (1985). 'Stripping away the rhetoric of protection: violence to women, law and the state in Britain and the USA'. *International Journal of the Sociology of Law,* 13, 4, 357-374.

Harris, R. N. and Bologh, R. W. (1985). 'The dark side of love: blue and white collar wife abuse'. *Victimology.* 10, 242-252.

Hecker, E. A. (1910). *A Short History of Women's Rights: From the Days of Augustus to the Present Time. London: Putnam's Sons.*

Herrington, L. H. (1986). *Family Violence: mistaken beliefs about the crime.* Paper presented to the United Nations Expert Group Meeting on Violence Within the Family with special emphasis on its effects on women. Vienna.

Homant, R. J. and Kennedy, D. B. (1985). 'Police perception of spouse abuse: a comparison of male and female officers'. *Journal of Criminal Justice,* 13, 29-47.

Home Office. (1986). *Statistics of Domestic Proceedings in Magistrates' Courts, England and Wales, 1985.* Home Office Statistical Bulletin 36/86. London: Government Statistical Service.

Homer, M. *et al.* (1985). 'The burden of dependency'. In: Johnson, N. (Ed.). (1985). *Marital Violence.* Sociological Review Monograph. London: Routledge and Kegan Paul.

Horley, S. (1988). 'A pioneering police plan to help battered women'. *Social Work Today,* March, 24.

Horton, C. and Smith, D. J. (1988) *Evaluating Police Work.* London: Policy Studies Institute.

Hotaling, G. T. (1980). 'Attribution processes in husband-wife violence'. In: Straus, M. A. and Hotaling, G. T. (1980). *The Social Causes of Husband-Wife Violence.* Minneapolis, Minnesota: University of Minnesota Press, 39-50.

Hough, J. M. and Mayhew, P. (1983). *The British Crime Survey: First Report.* Home Office Research Study 76. London: HMSO.

Hough, J. M. and Mayhew, P. (1985). *Taking Account of Crime: key findings from the 1984 British Crime Survey.* Home Office Research Study 85. London: HMSO.

House of Commons Select Committee on Violence in Marriage. HC 248, 1974-75.

Humphreys, J. C. and Humphreys, W. O. (1985). 'Mandatory arrest: a means of primary and secondary prevention of abuse of female partners'. *Victimology,* 10, 267-280.

Jaffe, P. and Burris, C. A. (1984). *An Integrated Response to Wife Assault: a community model.* Ottawa: Ministry of the Solicitor General.

Jaffe, P. and Thompson, J. (1978). 'The Family Consultant Service with the London Police Force'. In: Ekelaar, J. and Katz, S. (eds.) *Family violence: An International and Interdisciplinary Study.* Toronto: Butterworths.

Jaffe, P. and Thompson, J. (1982). *Family Consultant Service with the London Police Force. A Prescriptive Package.* Ottawa: Ministry of the Solicitor General.

Jaffe, P. and Thompson, J. (1984). 'Crisis Intervention on the London Family Consultant Model'. *RCMP Gazette.* 46(5 and 6), 1-8, 12-17.

Jaffe, P., Thompson, J. and Pacquin, M. (1978) 'Immediate family crisis intervention as preventative mental health: preliminary evaluation of the family consultant program'. *Professional Psychology.* 9, 551-560.

Jaffe, P., Thompson, J. and Wolfe, D. (1984). 'Evaluating the impact of a specialised civilian family crisis unit within a police force on the resolution of family conflicts'. *Journal of Preventive Pyschiatry,* 2, 1, 63-73.

Jaffe, P., Wolfe, D. A., Telford, A. and Austin, G. (1986a). 'The impact of police charges in incidents wife abuse'. *Journal of Family Violence,* 1, 1, 37-49.

Jaffe, P., Wolfe, D. A. Wilson, S. and Zak, L. (1986b). 'Emotional and physical health problems of battered women'. *Canadian Journal of Psychiatry.* 31, 625-629.

Jaffe, P., Wolfe, D. A., Wilson, S. and Zak, L. (1986c). 'Similarities in behavioural and social maladjustment among child victims and witnesses to family violence'. *American Journal of Orthopsychiatry.* 56, 1, 142-146.

Jesperson, A. (1987). '"The domestics" dilemma'. *Police Review,* 3 July, 1328-1329.

Johnson, N. (1985). 'Police, social work and medical responses to battered women'. In: Johnson, N., (ed.). *Marital Violence.* Sociological Review Monograph. London: Routledge and Kegan Paul.

Jolin A. (1983). 'Domestic violence legislation: an impact assessment'. *Journal of Police Science and Administration,* 11, 4, 451-456.

Jones, T. and Maclean, B. and Young, J. (1986). *The Islington Crime Survey.* Aldershot: Gower.

Judicial Statistics (1987). London: HMSO.

Kalmuss, D. S. (1984). 'Intergenerational transmission of marital aggression'. *Journal of Marriage and the Family.* February, 11-19.

Kalmuss, D. S. and Straus, M. A. (1981). 'A wife's marital dependency and wife abuse'. *Journal of Marriage and the Family.* (May), 277-286.

Kaufman Kantor, G. and Straus, M. A. (1987a). *Stopping The Violence: Battered Women, Police Utilisation and Police Response.* Paper presented to the American Society of Criminology Meeting, Montreal, November, 1987.

Kaufman Kantor, G. and Straus, M. A. (1987b). 'The drunken bum theory of wife-beating'. *Social Problems.* 34, 213-230.

Kennedy, D. B. and Homant, R. J. (1983). 'Attitudes of abused women toward male and female police officers'. *Criminal Justice Behaviour.* 10, 391-405.

Klein, D. (1982). 'Battered wives and the domination of women'. In: Rafter, N. H. and Stanko, E. (Eds.). (1982). *Judge, Lawyer, Victim, Thief: Women, Gender Roles and Criminal Justice.* Boston, Mass: Northeastern University Press.

La Fave, W. (1969). 'Non invocation of the criminal law by police'. In: Cressey, D. R. and Ward, D. (Eds.). *Delinquency, Crime and Social Process.* New York: Harper and Row.

Langan, P. and Innes, C. (1986). *Preventing Domestic Violence Against Women. Special Report.* US Bureau of Statistics, Department of Justice. Washington D.C.: Department of Justice.

Langley, R. and Levy, R. (1977). *Wife Beating: the silent crisis.* New York: E. P. Dutton.

Lasch, C. (1977). *Haven in a Heartless World: the family besieged.* New York: Basic Books.

Leibman, D. A. and Schwartz, J. A. (1972). 'Police programs in domestic crisis intervention'. In: Snibbe, J. R. and Snibbe, H. M. *The Urban Policeman in Transition.* Springfield, Mass.: Charles C. Thomas.

Lerette, P. (1984). *Study on the Restigouche Family Crisis Interveners Program.* Ottawa: Ministry of the Solicitor General.

Lerman, L. G. (1981). *Prosecution of Spouse Abuse. Innovations in Criminal Justice Response.* Washington D.C.: Centre for Woman's Policy Studies.

Levinger, G. (1966). 'Source of marital dissatisfaction among applicants for divorce'. *American Journal of Orthopsychiatry,* 36, 5, 803-807.

London Strategic Policy Unit, (1986). *Police Response to Domestic Violence.* Police Monitoring and Research Unit Briefing Paper 1. London: London Strategic Policy Unit.

L'orange, H. (1986). Untitled paper reviewing developments in New South Wales to reduce domestic violence presented at the United Nations Expert Group on Violence in the Family. Vienna.

Loving, N. and Farmer, M. (1980). *Responding to Spouse Abuse and Wife Beating: a guide for the police.* Washington D.C.: Police Executive Research Forum.

Loving, N. and Quirk, M. (1982). 'Spouse abuse: the need for new law enforcement responses'. *FBI Law Enforcement Bulletin,* 51/12, 10-16.

Macdonald, A. (1911). 'Death penalty and homicide'. *American Journal of Sociology,* 16, 96.

Macleod, L. (1987). *Battered But Not Beaten... Preventing Wife Battering in Canada.* Ottawa: Canadian Advisory Council on the Status of Women.

Macleod, M. (1983). 'Victim non co-operation in domestic disputes'. *Criminology,* 21, 3, 395-416.

Maidment, S. (1978). 'The law's response to marital violence'. In: Eckelaar, J. and Katz, S. (Eds.). *Family Violence: an International Interdisciplinary Study.* Canada: Butterworths.

Maidment, S. (1983). 'Civil v criminal: the use of legal remedies in responses to domestic violence in England and Wales'. *Victimology,* 8, 172-87.

Maidment, S. (1985). 'Domestic violence and the law: the 1976 Act and its aftermath'. In: Johnson, N. (Ed.). *Marital Violence*. Sociological Review Monograph No. 31. London: Routledge and Kegan Paul.

Marsden, D. (1978). 'Sociological perspectives on family violence'. In: Martin, J. P. (Ed.). (1978). *Violence in the Family.* Chichester: John Wiley.

Marsden, D. and Owen, D. (1975). 'Jekyll and Hyde marriages'. *New Society,* 8 May, 333.

Marshall, T. (1985). *Alternatives to Criminal Courts*. Aldershot: Gower.

Martin, D. (1976). *Battered Wives*. San Francisco: Glide Publications.

Martin, D. (1978). 'Battered women: society's problem'. In: Chapman, J. R., and Gates, M. *The Victimization of Women*. Beverly Hills, Calfornia: Sage.

Maynard, M. (1985). 'The response of social workers to domestic violence'. In: Pahl, J. (Ed.) *Private Violence and Public Policy*. London: Routledge and Kegan Paul.

McCabe, S. and Sutcliffe, F. (1978). *Defining Crime*. Oxford: Blackwell.

McClintock, F. (1963). *Crimes of Violence*. London: Macmillan.

McGregor, O. (1957). *Divorce in England*. London. Heinemann.

Melville, J. (1978). 'Some violent families.' In: Martin, J. P. (Ed.). *Violence and the Family*. Chichester: John Wiley.

Metropolitan Police (1986). *Report of the Working Party into Domestic Violence*. London: Metropolitan Police.

Moody, S. R. and Tombs, J. (1982). *Prosecutions in the Public Interest*. Edinburgh: Scottish Academic Press.

Moore, D. (1979). *Battered Women*. Beverly Hills: Sage.

Moore, J. G. (1975). 'Yo-yo children: victims of matrimonial violence'. *Child Welfare*. 54, 557-566.

Morash, M. (1986). 'Wife Battering'. *Criminal Justice Abstracts*. June 1986, 252-271.

Morgan, J. B. (1980). *The Police as Detectors of Crime*. Devon and Cornwall Constabulary.

Morris, A. (1987). *Women, Crime and Criminal Justice*. Oxford: Blackwell.

Murch, M., *et al.* (1987). *The Overlapping Family Jurisdiction of Magistrates' Courts and County Courts*. Bristol: Sociological Centre for Family Studies, University of Bristol.

Newburn, T. (1988). *The Use and Enforcement of Compensation Orders in Magistrates' Courts*. Home Office Research Study 102. London: HMSO.

Nuttall, S.E. *et al.* (1985). 'Wife battering: an emerging problem in public health'. *Canadian Journal of Public Health,* 76, 297-299.

O'Brien, J. E. (1971). 'Violence in divorce-prone families'. *Journal of Marriage and the Family.* 33, 4, 692-695.

Ontario Standing Committee on Social Development. (1983). *Family Violence: Wife Battering. Ontario Government Initiatives.* Toronto: Ontario Standing Committee on Social Development.

Ontario Status of Women Council. (1980). *Brief on Behalf of Battered Women.* Toronto: Status of Women Council.

Oppenlander, N. (1982). 'Coping or copping out?' Police service delivery in domestic disputes'. *Criminology,* 20, 3-4, 449-465.

Pagelow, M. D. (1981a). *Woman-Battering. Victims and Their Experiences.* Beverly Hills, California: Sage.

Pagelow, M. D. (1981b). 'Leaving Violent Relationships'. *Journal of Family Issues,* 2, 4, 391-414.

Pagelow, M. D. (1985). ''The battered husband syndrome'' social problem or much ado about little?'. In: Johnson, N. (Ed.). *Marital Violence.* London: Routledge and Kegan Paul.

Pahl, J. (1979). 'The general practitioner and the problems of battered women'. *Journal of Medical Ethics,* 5, 117-123.

Pahl, J. (1980). 'Patterns of money management within marriage'. *Journal of Social Policy,* 9, 313.

Pahl, J. (1982a). 'Police response to battered women'. *Journal of Social Welfare Law,* (November), 337-343.

Pahl, J. (1982b). 'Men who assault their wives: what can health visitors do to help'? *Health Visitor,* 55, 528-30.

Pahl, J. (Ed.). (1985). *Private Violence and Public Policy.* London: Routledge and Kegan Paul.

Parker, S. (1985). 'The legal background'. In: Pahl, J. (Ed). (1985). *Private Violence and Public Policy.* London: Routledge and Kegan Paul.

Parkinson, P. (1986). 'The Domestic Violence Act and Richards v Richards.' *Family Law,* 16, 70-73.

Parnas, R. (1967). 'The police response to the domestic disturbance' *Wisconsin Law Review,* Fall, 914.

Parnas, R. (1971). 'The police discretion and diversion of incidents of intra-family violence'. *Law and Contemporary Problems,* 36, 4, 539-565.

Parsloe, S. (1987). 'Battered by men and bruised by the law'. *The Law Magazine.* 4 September.

Pearce, J. B. and Snortum, J. R. (1983). 'Police effectiveness in handling disturbance calls: an evaluation of crises intervention training'. *Criminal Justice and Behaviour,* 10, 1, 71-92.

Pearl, D. (1986). 'Public housing allocation and domestic disputes'. In: Freeman, M. D. A. (Ed). *Essays in Family Law 1985. Current Legal Problems.* London: Sweet and Maxwell.

Pence, E. (1983). *The Law Enforcement and Criminal Justice System. An Intervention Model for Domestic Assault Cases.* Duluth, Minnesota: Police Department.

Pence, E. (1985). *Criminal Justice Response to Domestic Assault Cases: a guide for policy development.* Duluth, Mn.: Domestic Abuse Intervention Project, Minnesota Program Development Inc.

Piliavin, I. and Briar, S. (1969). 'Police encounters with juveniles'. In: Cressey, D. R. and Ward, D. (Eds.). Delinquency, Crime and Social Process. New York: Harper and Row.

Pizzey, E. (1974). *Scream Quietly or the Neighbours Will Hear.* Harmondsworth: Penguin.

Pizzey, E. and Shapiro, J. (1981). 'Choosing a violent relationship'. *New Society,* 23 April, 133.

Pizzey, E. and Shapiro, J. (1982). *Prone to Violence.* London: Hamlyn.

Pleck, E. (1987). *Domestic Tyranny. The Making of Social Policy Against Family Violence from Colonial Times to the Present.* New York: Oxford University Press.

Powell, G. and Magrath, C. (1985). *Police and Criminal Evidence Act 1984.* London: Longman Progressive.

Punch, M. and Naylor, T. (1973). 'The police. A social service'. *New Society,* 24 May, 358-361.

Radloff, L. S. and Rae, D. S. (1979). 'Components of the sex difference in depression: sex differences and similarities'. *Journal of Abnormal Psychology,* 88, 2, 174-181.

Radloff, L. S. and Cox, S. (1981). 'Sex differences in depression in relation to learned susceptabilities'. In: Cox, S. (Ed.). *Female Psychology: the emerging self.* New York: St Martin's Press. (2nd Edition.)

Reitz, W. (1974). 'Evaluation of police family crisis training and consultation'. *Canadian Police Chief.* 63, 3, 29-32.

Roy, M. (1977). *Battered Women.* New York: Van Nostrand Reinhold.

Roy, M. (1982). 'Four thousand partners in violence: a trend analysis'. In: Roy, M. (Ed.). *The Abusive Partner.* New York: Van Nostrand Reinhold.

Russell, D. (1982). *Rape in Marriage*. New York: Collier Books, Macmillan Publishing Co.

Sanders, A. (1987). *Prosecuting Domestic and Non-Domestic Violence*. Unpublished paper presented at British Criminology Conference, July, Sheffield.

Scheter, S. (1982). *Women and Male Violence*. London: Pluto Press.

Scott, E. (1981). *Calls for service: citizen demand and initial police response*. Washington D.C.: Government Printing Office.

Scott, P. D. (1974). 'Battered wives'. *British Journal of Psychiatry*, 125, (November) 433-441.

Scottish Women's Aid (1980). *Local Group Reports on Statistics*. Edinburgh: Scottish Women's Aid.

Seligman, M. (1975). *Helplessness: on depression, development and death*. San Francisco: Freeman.

Sherman, L. W. and Berk, R. A. (1984). 'The specific deterrent effects of arrest for domestic assault'. *American Sociological Review*, 49, 2, 261-272.

Sherman, L. W., Cohn, E. G. and Hamilton, E. E. (1986). *Police Policy on Domestic Violence: a national survey*. Washington D.C.: Crime Control Institute.

Sinclair, D. (1985). *Understanding Wife Assault: a training manual for counsellors and advocates*. Toronto: Ontario Government Bookstore.

Snell, J., Rosenwald, R. and Robey, A. (1964). 'The wifebeater's wife.' *Archives of General Psychiatry*, 11 (August), 107-112.

Sonkin, D. J. and Durphy, M. (1982). *Learning to Live Without Violence*. San Francisco: Volcano Press.

Southgate, P. (1986). *Police-Public Encounters*. Home Office Research Study No. 77. London: HMSO.

Stanko, E. A. (1985). *Intimate Intrusions. Women's Experience of Male Violence*. London: Routledge and Kegan Paul.

Stark, E., Flitcraft, A. and Frazier, W. (1979). 'Medicine and patriarchal violence: the social construction of a private event'. *International Journal of Health Services*, 9, 3, 461-493.

Status of Women, Ottawa. (1986). *Final Report of the Federal, Provincial, Territorial Working Group on Wife Battering*. Ottawa: Status of Women.

Steinmetz, S. K. and Straus, M. A. (1974). *Violence in the family*. New York: Harper and Row.

Storr, A. (1974). *Human Aggression*. Harmondsworth: Penguin.

Straus, M. A. (1974). 'Leveling, civility and violence in the family' *Journal of Marriage and the Family*, 36, February 13-30.

Straus, M. A. (1976). 'Sexual inequality, cultural norms, and wife-beating'. In: Chapman, J. R. and Gates, M. (Eds.). *Women into Wives: the legal and economic impact of marriage.* Sage Yearbooks in Women's Policy Studies, Vol. 2. Beverly Hills, California: Sage.

Straus, M. A. (1977a). *Normative and Behavioural Aspects of Violence between Spouses.* Paper presented at Symposium on violence in Canadian Society. Simon Fraser University, British Columbia, March 1977.

Straus, M. A. (1977b). 'A sociological perspective on the prevention and treatment of wife-beating'. In: Roy, M. (Ed.). *Battered Women. New York: Van Nostrand Reinhold,* pp 194-239.

Straus, M. A. (1980a). 'A sociological perspective on the causes of family violence'. In: Green, M. R. (Ed.). *Violence and the Family.* Boulder, Colorado: Westview Press.

Straus, M. A. (1980b). 'Sexual inequality and wife beating'. In: Strauss, M. A. and Hotaling, G. T. (1980). *The Social Causes of Husband-Wife Violence.* Minneapolis, Minnesota: University of Minnesota Press.

Straus, M. A. (1980c). 'The marriage license as a hitting license: evidence from popular culture, law and social science'. In: Straus, M. A. and Hotaling, G. T. (1980). *The Social Causes of Husband-Wife violence.* Minneapolis, Minnesota: University of Minnesota Press.

Straus, M. A. (1980d). 'Victims and aggressors in marital violence'. *American Behavioural Scientist,* 23, 5, 681-704.

Straus, M. A. (1983). 'Ordinary violence, child abuse and wife beating: what do they have in common?' In: Finkelhor, D., *et al.* (Eds.). *The Dark Side of Families.* Beverly Hills: Sage.

Straus, M. A. (1987). *Social Stratification, Social Bonds and Wife Beating in the United States.* Paper presented to the American Society of Criminology Meeting, Montreal, November.

Straus, M. A. and Gelles, R. (1986). 'Societal Change and Change in Family Violence, 1975 to 1985, as revealed in two national surveys'. *Journal of Marriage and the Family,* 48, August, 465-479.

Straus, M. A., Gelles, R. and Steinmetz, S. K. (1978). *Physical Violence in a Nationally Representative Sample of American Families.* Paper presented at the 9th World Congress on Sociology, Uppsala, Sweden, August 1978.

Straus, M. A., Gelles, R. and Steinmetz, S. K. (1980). *Behind Closed Doors.* New York: Anchor.

United States Attorney General's Task Force on Violence in the Family. (1984) *Final Report.*

United States Commission on Civil Rights. (1983). *Under the Rule of Thumb: battered women and the administration of justice.* Washington D.C.: United States Government Printing Press.

United States Department of Justice. (1983). *Report to the Nation on Crime and Justice: The Data.* Washington D.C.: Bureau of Justice Statistics.

United States Law Enforcement Assistance Administration. (1981). The Report from the Conference on Intervention Program for Men Who Batter. Washington D.C.: US Government Printing Office.

United States Police Foundations (1976). *Domestic Violence and the Police: Studies in Detroit and Kansas City.* Washington D.C.: Police Foundation.

Wachtel, A. and Levens, B. (1984). *Vancouver Therapy Groups for Assaulting Males: a programme development review.* Ottawa: Ministry of the Solicitor General.

Walker, L. E. (1976). 'Treatment alternatives for battered women'. In: Chapman, J. R. and Gates, M. (Eds.). *The Victimization of Women.* Beverly Hills, California: Sage.

Walker, L. E. (1978). 'Battered women and learned helplessness'. *Victimology.* 2, 3-4. 525-534.

Walker, L. E. (1979). *The Battered Woman.* New York: Harper and Row.

Walker, L. E. (1984). *The Battered Woman Syndrome.* New York: Springer.

Walker, L. E. (1985). 'Psychological impact of the criminalization of domestic violence on victims'. *Victimology,* 10, 281-300.

Wasik, M. (1983). 'Criminal injuries compensation and family violence'. *Journal of Social Welfare Law.* March, 100-108.

Wasoff, F. (1982). 'Legal protection from wife-beating: the processing of domestic assaults by Scottish prosecutors and criminal courts'. *International Journal of Sociology of Law,* 10, 2, 187-204.

Welsh Women's Aid. (1980). *Which Venue Now?* Cardiff: Welsh Women's Aid.

Wilson, E. (1983). *What Is To Be Done About Violence Against Women.* Harmondsworth: Penguin.

Wilt, J. and Bannon, J. (1977). *Domestic Violence and the Police. Studies in Detroit and Kansas City.* Washington D.C.: Police Foundation.

Wolfe, D. A., Jaffe, P., Wilson, S. and Zak, L. (1985). 'Children of battered women: the relation between child behaviour, family violence and maternal stress'. *Journal of Consulting and Clinical Psychology,* 55, 5, 657-665.

Wolfgang, M. E. (1958). *Patterns in Criminal Homicide.* New York: John Wiley.

Women's National Commission, (1985). *Violence against Women.* Report of an ad hoc working group. London: Cabinet Office.

Wood, D. (1986). Untitled paper presented at the United Nations Expert Group on Violence in the Family. Vienna.

Worral, A. and Pease, K. (1986). 'Personal crime against women: evidence from the 1982 British Crime Survey'. *Howard Journal.* 25, 2, 118-124.

Publications

Titles already published for the Home Office

Studies in the Causes of Delinquency and the Treatment of Offenders (SCDTO)

1. Prediction Methods in relation to borstal training. Hermann Mannheim and Leslie T. Wilkins, 1955. viii+2276pp. (11 340051 9).
2. *Time spent awaiting trial. Evelyn Gibson. 1960. v+45pp. (34-368-2).
3. *Delinquent generations. Leslie T. Wilkins. 1960. vi+20pp. (11 340053 5).
4. *Murder. Evelyn Gibson and S. Klein. 1961. iv+44pp. (11 340054 3).
5. Persistent criminals. A study of all offenders liable to preventive detention in 1956. W. H. Hammond and Edna Chayen. 1963. ix+237pp. (34-368-5).
6. *Some statistical and other numerical techniques for classifying individuals, P McNaughton-Smith. 1965. v+33pp. (34-368-6).
7. Probation research: a preliminary report. Part I. General outline of research. Part II. Study of Middlesex probation area (SOMPA). Steven Folkard, Kate Lyon, Margaret M. Carver and Erica O'Leary. 1966. vi+58pp. (11 340374 7).
8. *Probation research: national study of probation. Trends and regional comparisons in probation (England and Wales). Hugh Barr and Erica O'Leary. 1966. vii+51pp. (34-368-8).
9. *Probation Research. A survey of group work in the probation service. Hugh Barr. 1966. vii+94pp. (34-368-9).
10. *Types of delinquency and home background. A validation study of Hewitt and Jenkins' hypothesis. Elizabeth Field. 1967. vi+21pp. (34-368-10).
11. *Studies of female offenders. No. 1—Girls of 16-20 years sentenced to borstal or detention centre training in 1963. No. 2—Women offenders in the Metropolitan Police District in March and April 1957. No. 3—A description of women in prison on January 1, 1965. Nancy Goodman and Jean Price. 1967. v+78pp. (34-368-11).
12. *The use of the Jesness Inventory on a sample of British probationers. Martin Davies. 1967. iv+20pp. (34-368-12).
13. *The Jesness Inventory: application to approved school boys. Joy Mott. 1969. iv+27pp. (11 340063 2).

Home Office Research Studies (HORS)

1. *Workloads in children's departments. Eleanor Grey. 1969. vi+75pp. (11 340101 9).
2. Probationers in their social environment. A study of male probationers aged 17-20, together with an analysis of those reconvicted within twelve months. Martin Davies. 1969. vii+204pp. (11 340102 7).
3. *Murder 1957 to 1968. A Home Office Statistical Division report on murder in England and Wales. Evelyn Gibson and S. Klein (with annex by the Scottish Home and Health Department on murder in Scotland). 1969. vi+94pp. (11 340103 5).
4. *Firearms in crime. A Home Office Statistical report on indictable offences involving firearms in England and Wales. A. D. Weatherhead and B. M. Robinson. 1970. viii+39pp. (11 340104 3).
5. *Financial penalties and probation. Martin Davies. 1970. vii+39pp. (11 340105 1).
6. *Hostels for probationers. A study of the aims, working and variations in effectiveness of male male probation hostels with special reference to the influence of the environment on delinquency. Ian Sinclair. 1971. ix+200pp. (11 340106 X).

---

* Out of Print.

7. *Prediction methods in criminology—including a prediction study of young men on probation. Frances H. Simon. 1971. xi+234pp. (11 340107 8).

8. *Study of the juvenile liaison scheme in West Ham 1961-65. Marilyn Taylor. 1971. vi+46pp. (11 340108 6).

9. *Exploration in after-care. 1—After-care units in London, Liverpool and Manchester. Martin Silberman (Royal London Prisoners' Aid Society) and Brenda Chapman. II—After-care hostels receiving a Home Office grant. Ian Sinclair and David Snow (HORU). III—St. Martin of Tours House, Ayreh Leissner (National Bureau for Co-operation in Child Care). 1971. xi+140pp. (11 340109 4).

10. A survey of adoption in Great Britain. Eleanor Grey in collaboration with Roland M. Blunden. 1971. ix+168pp. (11 340110 8).

11. *Thirteen-year-old approved school boys in 1962. Elizabeth Field, W. H. Hammond and J. Tizard, 1971. xi+46pp. (11 340111 6).

12. Absconding from approved schools R. V. G. Clarke and D. N. Martin. 1971. vi+146pp. (11 340112 4).

13. An experiment in personality assessment of young men remanded in custody. H. Sylvia Anthony. 1972. viii+79pp. (11 340113 2).

14. *Girl offenders aged from 17-20 years. 1—Statistics relating to girl offenders aged 17-20 years from 1960 to 1970. II—Re-offending by girls released from borstals or detention centre training. III—The problems of girls released from borstal training during their period on after-care. Jean Davis and Nancy Goodman. 1972. v+77pp. (11 340114 0).

15. *The Controlled trial in institutional research-paradigm or pitfall for penal evaluators? R. V. G. Clarke and D. B. Cornish. 1972. v+33pp. (11 340115 9).

16. *A survey of fine enforcement. Paul Softley. 1973. v+65pp. (11 340116 7).

17. *An index of social environment—designed for use in social work research. Martin Davies. 1973. vi+63pp. (11 340117 5).

18. *Social enquiry reports and the probation service. Martin Davies and Andrea Knopf. 1973. v+49pp. (11 340118 3).

19. *Depression, psychopathic personality and attempted suicide in a borstal sample. H. Sylvia Anthony. 1973. viii+44pp. (11 340119 1).

20. *The use of bail and custody by London magistrates' courts before and after the Criminal Justice Act 1967. Frances Simon and Mollie Weatheritt. 1974. vi+78pp (11 340120 5).

21. Social work in the environment. A study of one aspect of probation practice. Martin Davies, with Margaret Rayfield, Alaster Calder and Tony Fowles. 1974. ix+151pp. (11 340121 3).

22. Social work in prison. An experiment in the use of extended contact with offenders. Margaret Shaw. 1974. vii+154pp. (11 340122 1).

23. Delinquency amongest opiate users. Joy Mott and Marilyn Taylor. 1974. vi+31pp. (11 340663 0).

24. IMPACT. Intensive matched probation and after-care treatment. Vol. I—The Design of the probation experiment and an interim evaluation. M. S. Folkard, A. J. Fowles, B.C. McWilliams, W. McWilliams, D. D. Smith, D. E. Smith and G. R. Walmsley. 1974. v+54pp. (11 340664 9).

25. The approved school experience. An account of boys' experiences of training under differing regimes of approved schools, with an attempt to evaluate the effectiveness of that training. Anne B. Dunlop. 1974. vii+124pp. (11 340665 7).

26. *Absconding from open prisons. Charlotte Banks, Patricia Mayhew and R. J. Sapsford. 1975. vii+89pp. (11 340666 5).

27. Driving while disqualified. Sue Kriefman. 1975. vi+136pp. (11 340667 3).

28. Some male offenders' problems. I—homeless offenders in Liverpool. W. McWilliams. II—Casework with short-term prisoners. Julie Holborn. 1975. x+147pp. (11 340668 1).

29. *Community service orders. K. Pease, P. Durkin, I. Earnshaw, D. Payne and J. Thorpe. 1975. viii+80pp. (11 340669 X).

30. Field Wing Bail Hostel: the first nine months. Frances Simon and Sheena Wilson. 1975. viii+55pp. (11 340670 3).

---

* Out of Print.

31. Homicide in England and Wales 1967-1971. Evelyn Gibson. 1975. iv+59pp. (11 340753 X).

32. Residential treatment and its effects on delinquency. D. B. Cornish and R. V. G. Clarke. 1975. vi+74pp. (11 340672 X).

33. Further studies of female offenders. Part A: Borstal girls eight years after release. Nancy Goodman, Elizabeth Maloney and Jean Davies. Part B: The sentencing of women at the London Higher Courts. Nancy Goodman, Paul Durkin and Janet Halton. Part C: Girls appearing before a juvenile court. Jean Davies. 1976. vi+114pp. (11 340673 8).

34. *Crime as opportunity. P. Mayhew, R. V. G. Clarke, A. Sturman and J. M. Hough. 1976. vii+36pp. (11 340674 6).

35. The effectiveness of sentencing: a review of the literature. S. R. Brody. 1976. v+89pp. (11 340675 4).

36. IMPACT. Intensive matched probation and after-care treatment. Vol II—The results of the experiment. M. S. Folkard, D. E. Smith and D. D. Smith. 1976. xi+400pp. (11 340676 2).

37. Police cautioning in England and Wales. J. A. Ditchfield. 1976. vi+31pp. (11 340677 2).

38. Parole in England and Wales. C. P. Nuttall, with E. E. Barnard, A. J. Fowles, A. Frost, W. H. Hammond, P. Mayhew, K. Pease, R. Tarling and M. J. Weatheritt. 1977. vi+90pp. (11 340678 9).

39. Community service assessed in 1976. K. Pease, S. Billingham and I. Earnshaw. 1977. vi+29pp. (11 340679 7).

40. Screen violence and film censorship: a review of research. Stephen Brody. 1977. vii+179pp. (11 340680 0).

41. Absconding from borstals. Gloria K. Laycock. 1977. v+82pp. (11 340681 9).

42. Gambling: a review of the literature and its implications for policy and research. D. B. Cornish. 1978. xii+284pp. (11 340682 7).

43. Compensation orders in magistrates' courts. Paul Softley. 1978. v+41pp. (11 340683 5).

44. Research in criminal justice. John Croft. 1978. iv+16pp. (11 340684 3).

45. Prison welfare: an account of an experiment at Liverpool. A. J. Fowles. 1978. v+34pp. (11 340685 1).

46. Fines in magistrates' courts. Paul Softley. 1978. v+42pp. (11 340686 X).

47. Tackling vandalism. R. V. G. Clarke (editor), F. J. Gladstone, A. Sturman and Sheena Wilson (contributors). 1978. vi+91pp. (11 340687 8).

48. Social inquiry reports: a survey. Jennifer Thorpe. 1979. vi+55pp. (11 340688 6).

49. Crime into public view. P. Mayhew, R. V. G. Clarke, J. N. Burroughs, J. M. Hough and S. W. C. Winchester. 1979. v+36pp. (11 340689 4).

50. *Crime and the community. John Croft. 1979. v+16pp. (11 340690 8).

51. Life-sentence prisoners. David Smith (editor), Christopher Brown, Joan Worth, Roger Sapsford and Charlotte Banks (contributors). 1979. iv+51pp. (11 340691 6).

52. Hostels for offenders. Jane E. Andrews, with an appendix by Bill Sheppard. 1979. v+30pp. (11 340692 4).

53. Previous convictions, sentence and reconviction: a statistic study of a sample of 5,000 offenders convicted January 1971. G. J. O. Phillpotts and L. B. Lancucki. 1979. v+55pp. (11 340693 2).

54. Sexual offences, consent and sentencing. Roy Walmsley and Karen White. 1979. vi+77pp. (11 340694 0).

55. Crime prevention and the police. John Burrows, Paul Ekblom and Kevin Heal. 1979. v+37pp. (11 340695 9).

56. Sentencing practice in magistrates' courts. Roger Tarling, with the assistance of Mollie Weatheritt. 1979. vii+54pp. (11 340696).

57. Crime and comparative research. John Croft. 1979. iv+16pp. (11 340697 5).

58. Race, crime and arrests. Philip Stevens and Carole F. Willis. 1979. v+69pp. (11 340698 3).

59. Research and criminal policy. John Croft. 1980. iv+14pp. (11 340699 1).

60. Junior attendance centres. Anne B. Dunlop. 1980. v+49pp. (11 340700 9).

---

* Out of Print.

61. Police interrogation: an observational study in four police stations. Paul Softley, with the assistance of David Brown, Bob Forde, George Mair and David Moxon. 1980. vii+67pp. (11 340701 7).

62. Co-ordinating crime prevention efforts. F. J. Gladstone. 1980. v+74pp. (11 340702 5).

63. Crime prevention publicity: an assessment. D. Riley and P. Mayhew. 1980. v+47pp. (11 340703 3).

64. Taking offenders out of circulation. Stephen Brody and Roger Tarling. 1980. v+46pp. (11 340704 1).

65. *Alcoholism and social policy: are we on the right lines? Mary Tuck. 1980. v+30pp. (11 340705 X).

66. Persistent petty offenders. Suzan Fairhead. 1981. vi+78pp. (11 340706 8).

67. Crime control and the police. Pauline Morris and Kevin Heal. 1981. v+71pp. (11 340707 6).

68. Ethnic minorities in Britain: a study of trends in their positions since 1961. Simon Field, George Mair, Tom Rees and Philip Stevens. 1981. v+48pp. (11 340708 4).

69. Managing criminological research. John Croft. 1981. iv+17pp. (11 340709 2).

70. Ethnic minorities, crime and policing: a survey of the experiences of West Indians and whites. Mary Tuck and Peter Southgate. 1981. iv+54pp. (11 340765 3).

71. Contested trials in magistrates' courts. Julie Vennard. 1982. v+32pp. (11 340766 1).

72. Public disorder: a review of research and a study in one inner city area. Simon Field and Peter Southgate. 1982. v+77pp. (11 340767 X).

73. Clearing up crime. John Burrows and Roger Tarling. 1982. vii+31pp. (11 340768 8).

74. Residential burglary: the limits of prevention. Stuart Winchester and Hilary Jackson. 1982. v+47pp. (11 340769 6).

75. Concerning crime. John Croft. 1982. iv+16pp. (11 340770 X).

76. The British Crime Survey: First Report, Mike Hough and Pat Mayhew. 1983. v+62pp. (11 340789 6).

77. Contacts between police and public: findings from the British Crime Survey. Peter Southgate and Paul Ekblom. 1984. v+42pp. (11 340771 8).

78. Fear of crime in England and Wales. Michael Maxfield. 1984. v+51pp. (11 340772 6).

79. Crime and police effectiveness. Ronald V. Clarke and Mike Hough. 1984. ib+33pp. (11 340773 4).

80. The attitudes of ethnic minorities. Simon Field. 1984. v+50pp. (11 340077 2).

81. Victims of crime: the dimensions of risk. Michael Gottfriedson. 1984. v+54pp. (11 340775 0).

82. The tape recording of police interviews with suspects: an interim report. Carole Willis. 1984. v+45pp. (11 340776 9).

83. Parental supervision and juvenile delinquency. David Riley and Margaret Shaw. 1985. v+90pp. (11 340799 8).

84. Adult prisons and prisoners in England and Wales 1970-82: a review of the findings of social research. Joy Mott. 1985. vi+73pp. (11 340801 3).

85. Taking account of crime: key findings from the 1984 British Crime Survey. Mike Hough and Pat Mayhew. 1985. vi+115pp. (11 340810 2).

86. Implementing crime prevention measures. Tim Hope. 1985. vi+82pp. (11 340812 9).

87. Resettling refugees: the lessons of research. Simon Field. 1985. vi+62pp. (11 340815 3).

88. Investigating burglary: the measurement of police performance. John Burrows. 1986. v+36pp. (11 340824 2).

89. Personal violence. Roy Walmsley. 1986. vi+87pp. (11 340827 7).

90. Police public encounters. Peter Southgate with the assistance of Paul Ekblom. 1986. vi+150pp. (11 340834 X).

91. Grievance procedures in prisons. John Ditchfield and Claire Austin. 1986. vi+78pp. (11 340839 0).

92. The effectiveness of the Forensic Science Service. Malcolm Ramsay. 1987. v+100pp. (11 340842 0).

---

* Out of Print

93. The police complaints procedure: a survey of complainants' views. David Brown. 1987. v+98pp. (11 340853 6).
94. The validity of the reconviction prediction score, Denis Ward. 1987. vi+40pp. (11 340682 X).
95. Economic aspects of the illicit drug market and drug enforcement policies in the United Kingdom Adam Wagstaff and Alan Maynard. 1988. vii+156pp. (11 340883 8).
96. Schools, disruptive behaviour and delinquency: a review of research. John Graham. 1988. v+70pp. (11 340887 0).
97. The tape-recording of police interviews with suspects: a second interim report. Carole Willis, John Macleod and Peter Naish. 1988. vii+97pp. (11 340888 9).
98. Triable-either-way cases: Crown Court or magistrates' court? David Riley and Julie Vennard. 1988. v+52pp. (11 340890 0).
99. Directing patrol work: a study of uniformed policing. John Burrows and Helen Lewis. 1988. v+66pp. (11 340891 9).
100. Probation day centres, George Mair. 1988. v+44pp. (11 340894 3).
101. Amusement machines: dependency and delinquency. John Graham. 1988. v+48pp. (11 340895 1).
102. The use of enforcement of compensation orders in magistrates' courts. Tim Newburn. 1988. v+48pp. (11 340896 X).
103. Sentencing practice in the Crown Court. David Moxon. 1988. v+90pp. (11 340902 8).
104. Detention at the police station under the Police and Criminal Evidence Act 1984. David Brown. 1989. v+76pp. (0 11 340908 7).
105. Changes in rape offences and sentencing. Charles Lloyd and Roy Walmsley. 1989. vi+53pp. (0 11 340910 9).
106. Concerns about rape. Lorna J.F. Smith. 1989. v+48pp (0 11 340911 7).

ALSO

Designing out crime. R.V.G. Clarke and P. Mayhew (editors). 1980. vii+186pp. (22 340732 7).
(This book collects, with an introduction, studies that were originally published in HORS 34, 47, 49, 55, 62 and 63 and which are illustrative of the situational approach to crime prevention.)
Policing today. Kevin Heal, Roger Tarling and John Burrows (editors). 1985. v+181pp. (11 340800 5).
(This book brings together twelve separate studies on police matters produced during the last few years by the unit. The collection records some relatively little known contributions to the debate on policing.)
Managing criminal justice: a collection of papers. David Moxon (editor). 1985. vi+222pp. (11 340811 0).
(This book brings together a number of studies bearing on the management of the criminal justice system. It includes papers by social scientists and operational researchers working within the Research and Planning Unit, and academic researchers who have studied particular aspects of the criminal process.)
Situational crime prevention: from theory into practice. Kevin Heal and Gloria Laycock (editors). 1986. vii+166pp. (11 340826 9).
(Following the publication of *Designing out crime*, further research has been completed on the theoretical background to crime prevention. In drawing this work together this book sets down some of the theoretical concerns and discusses the emerging practical issues. It includes contributions by Unit staff as well as academics from this country and abroad.)
Communities and crime reduction. Tim Hope and Margaret Shaw (editors). 1988. vii+311pp. (11 340892 7).
(The central theme of this book is the possibility of preventing crime by building upon the resources of local communities and of active citizens. The specially commissioned chapters, by distinguished international authors, review contemporary research and policy on community crime prevention.)
New directions in police training. Peter Southgate (editor). 1988. xi+256pp. (11 340889 7).
(Training is central to the development of the police role, and particular thought and effort now go into making it more responsive to current needs—in order to produce police officers who are both effective and sensitive in their dealings with the public. This book illustrates some of the thinking and research behind these developments.)

DOMESTIC VIOLENCE

The above HMSO publications can be purchased from Government Bookshops or through booksellers.

The following Home Office research publications are available on request from the Home Office Research and Planning Unit, 50 Queen Anne's Gate, London, SW1H 9AT.

Research Unit Papers (RUP)
1. Uniformed police work and management technology. J. M. Hough. 1980.
2. Supplementary information on sexual offences and sentencing. Roy Walmsley and Karen White. 1980.
3. Board of Visitor adjudications. David Smith, Claire Austin and John Ditchfield. 1981.
4. Day centres and probations. Suzan Fairhead, with the assistance of J. Wilkinson-Grey. 1981.

Research and Planning Unit Papers (RPUP)
5. Ethnic minorities and complaints against the police. Philip Stevens and Carole Willis. 1982.
6. *Crime and public housing. Mike Hough and Pat Mayhew (editors). 1982.
7. *Abstracts of race relations research. George Mair and Philip Stevens (editors). 1982.
8. Police probationer training in race relations. Peter Southgate. 1982.
9. *The police response to calls from the public. Paul Ekblom and Kevin Heal. 1982.
10. City centre crime: a situational approach to prevention. Malcolm Ramsay. 1982.
11. Burglary in schools: the prospects for prevention. Tim Hope. 1982.
12. *Fine enforcement. Paul Softley and David Moxon. 1982.
13. Vietnamese refugees. Peter Jones. 1982.
14. Community resources for victims of crime. Karen Williams, 1983.
15. The use, effectiveness and impact of police stop and search powers. Carole Willis. 1983.
16. Acquittal rates. Sid Butler. 1983.
17. Criminal justice comparisons: the case of Scotland and England and Wales. Lorna J. F. Smith. 1983.
18. Time taken to deal with juveniles under criminal proceedings. Catherine Frankenburg and Roger Tarling. 1983.
19. Civilian review of complaints against the police: a survey of the United States literature. David C. Brown. 1983.
20. Police action on motoring offences. David Riley. 1983.
21. *Diverting drunks from the criminal justice system. Sue Kingsley and George Mair. 1983.
22. The staff resource implications of an independent prosecution system. Peter R. Jones. 1983.
23. Reducing the prison population: an explanatory study in Hampshire. David Smith, Bill Sheppard, George Mair and Karen Williams. 1984.
24. Criminal justice system model: magistrates' courts sub-model. Susan Rice. 1984.
25. Measures of police effectiveness and efficiency. Ian Sinclair and Clive Miller. 1984.
26. Punishment practice by prison Boards of Visitors. Susan Iles, Adrienne Connors, Chris May and Joy Mott. 1984.
27. *Reparation, conciliation and mediation. Tony Marshall. 1984.
28. Magistrates' domestic courts: new perspectives. Tony Marshall (editor). 1984.
29. Racism awareness training for the police. Peter Southgate. 1984.
30. Community constables: a study of policing initiative. David Brown and Susan Iles. 1985.
31. Recruiting volunteers. Hilary Jackson. 1985.
32. Juvenile sentencing: is there a tariff? David Moxon, Peter Jones and Roger Tarling. 1985.

* Out of Print.

33. Bring people together: mediation and reparation projects in Great Britain. Tony Marshall and Martin Walpole. 1985.

34. Remands in the absence of the accused. Chris May. 1985.

35. Modelling the criminal justice system. Patricia M. Morgan. 1986.

36. The criminal justice system model: the flow model. Hugh Pullinger. 1986.

37. Burglary: police actions and victims' views. John Burrows. 1986.

38. Unlocking community resources: four experimental government small grant schemes. Hilary Jackson. 1986.

39. The cost of discriminating: a review of the literature. Shirley Dex. 1986.

40. Waiting for Crown Court trial: the remand population. Rachel Pearce. 1987.

41. Children's evidence: the need for corroboration. Carol Hedderman. 1987.

42. A preliminary study of victim offender mediation and reparation schemes in England and Wales. Gwynn Davis, Jacky Boucherat and David Watson. 1987.

43. Explaining fear of crime: evidence from the 1984 British Crime Survey. Michael Maxfield. 1988.

44. Judgements of crime seriousness: evidence from the 1984 British Crime Survey. Ken Pease, 1988.

45. Waiting time on the day in magiatrates' courts: a review of case listing practices. David Moxon and Roger Tarling (editors). 1988.

46. Bail and probation work: the ILPS temporary bail action project. George Mair. 1988.

47. Police work and manpower allocation. Roger Tarling. 1988.

48. Computers in the courtroom. Carol Hedderman. 1988.

49. Data interchange between magistrates' courts and other agencies. Carol Hedderman. 1988.

50. Bail and probation work: II; the use of London probation/bail hostels for bailees. Helen Lewis and George Mair. 1989.

* Out of Print.

DOMESTIC VIOLENCE

Research Bulletin

The Research Bulletin is published twice a year and consists mainly of short articles relating to projects which are part of the Home Office Research and Planning Unit's research programme.

Printed in the United Kingdom for HMSO.
Dd 292857, 5/90, C7